The Three Musketeers

James DeVita

SAMUEL FRENCH

FOUNDED 1830

SAMUELFRENCH.COM
SAMUELFRENCH-LONDON.CO.UK

FOR PRODUCTION ENQUIRIES

UNITED STATES AND CANADA
Info@SamuelFrench.com
1-866-598-8449

UNITED KINGDOM AND EUROPE
Plays@SamuelFrench-London.co.uk
020-7255-4302

Each title is subject to availability from Samuel French, depending upon country of performance. Please be aware that *THE THREE MUSKETEERS* may not be licensed by Samuel French in your territory. Professional and amateur producers should contact the nearest Samuel French office or licensing partner to verify availability.

NOTE

The originating theater should receive program credit in all future productions of the play substantially as follows:

"Originally commissioned by American Players Theater, developed and first performed by Madison Repertory Theater in a co-production with UW Theater, Madison, Wisconsin."

CHARACTERS

KING LOUIS XIII
D'ARTAGNAN
ATHOS
ARAMIS
PORTHOS
MONSIEUR TREVILLE
PLANCHET - servant to d'Artagnan
CARDINAL RICHELIEU
ROCHEFORT - a Cardinalist
JUSSAC - a Cardinalist
BICARAT - a Cardinalist
CAHUSAC - a Cardinalist
MILADY - of the Cardinal
KITTY
QUEEN ANNE OF AUSTRIA
CONSTANCE BONACIEUX
DONA ESTEFANA
GEORGE VILLIERS, DUKE OF BUCKINGHAM
MONSIEUR BONACIEUX
CHESNAYE - valet to the King
D'ARTAGNAN'S MOTHER
D'ARTAGNAN'S FATHER
GUARD 1 - Cardinalist
GUARD 2 - Cardinalist
LORD DE WINTER - Milady's brother-in-law
COUNT DE WARDES
JOHN FELTON - Lieutenant in the British Navy
6 MUSKETEERS
CAPTAIN
PASSENGER
HOSTESS

2 SERVANTS
A NUN
PATRICK - of the Duke of Buckingham
REILLY - of the Duke of Buckingham
JACKSON - of the Duke of Buckingham
A BRITISH OFFICER
AN ENGLISH NOBLEMAN
AN EXECUTIONER
LADIES IN WAITING
LORDS IN ATTENDANCE

The first production at the Madison Repertory Theater used twenty-six actors. The doubling they used was as follows:

Musketeer 5, Chesnaye, Captain, Messenger 2
Bonacieux, English Nobleman, Guest at ball
Father, Bicarat, Guest
Treville, Passenger, Messenger 1
Aramis, Guest
Musketeer 1, De Wardes, Guest, British Officer
Mother, Dona Estefana, Passenger, Nun 1
Cahusac, Recruit, Guest
Queen Anne, Nun 2
Guard 1, Musketeer 6, Patrick, Guest
Hostess, Mother Superior
Musketeer 3, Buckingham, Executioner
DeWinter, Musketeer 2
Guard 2, Musketeer 4, Jackson, Servant to Milady, Guest
Reilly, Guest, Felton, Servant to the King
Planchet, Guest
Kitty, Nun 3

THE THREE MUSKETEERS

ACT I

Scene 1

(The time: April 1625. A time of frequent war, riots and unrest. d'Artagnan and his father enter, midswordfight. After the fight it established, and during a particularly violent phrase, d'Art.'s mother enters with luggage. As she crosses the line of the fight, the men pause for a moment to let her pass, and then continue. After another short phrase or two, she enters again with doublet, towel, and another item or two.)

MOTHER *(As they continue fighting).* That's enough now. Enough! It's time to go.

D'ART. Yes, mother!

FATHER. In a moment!

MOTHER. It's getting late! I don't want him on the road after dark!

FATHER. Yes, yes, all right! *(To d'Art.)* Again! *(They finish another phrase and then stop. To d'Art.)* If you parry wide, like so, beat the thrust aside with your left hand. Better hazard a little hurt of the hand, than a thrust through the heart.

D'ART. Yes, father.

MOTHER *(Tossing a towel to d'Art).* Clean yourself up. *(To Father.)* You too.

FATHER. Oh, do stop. Bid Bejart lead my horse into the field.

MOTHER. I have already.

D'ART. My small bag, mother, did you - ?

MOTHER. Behind you. *(d'Artagnan checks his bags.)*

FATHER. And my - did you bring the - ?

MOTHER. Yes.

FATHER. Very well.

D'ART. So.

MOTHER *(Helping d'Art. on with his doublet)*. Be a good man, and stay safe.

FATHER. Never fear a quarrel.

MOTHER. Be gentle to women.

FATHER. Seek out adventures.

MOTHER *(To Father)*. Monsieur, please? *(To d'Art.)* Find profit in all that happens to you. Live happily and long. *(To father.)* Monsieur.

FATHER. Take no insult from any man. Remember it is by courage alone that a man makes his way in the world today.

MOTHER. Your father's advice might well warrant the rather frequent use of this. *(Gives d'Art. a jar.)* Apply it liberally for three days and it will cure any wound that hasn't reached the heart. *(Encouraging Father.)* You're father has something else to say to you.

FATHER. Yes. Yes, I do. I have not much to give you, son, save my horse and a few crowns - and this letter. Mark me, it is a letter - where's the letter? What did I do with the - ?! *(Mother hands him the letter.)* Thank you. Mark me, it is a letter of introduction to Monsieur Treville, Captain of the Royal Musketeers. We once were neighbors and we fought together under our last King. He began in life as you begin now, from this very town. Go to him with this letter, make him your model that you may, perchance, one day do as he has done.

D'ART. *(Receiving the letter.)* Thank you, sir.

FATHER. Be brave. You ought to be; you're a Gascon - and you're my son. *(Mother reminds him.)* Oh, yes. *(Presenting his sword.)* This is yours. Wear it well.

D'ART *(Truly moved)*. Sir.

FATHER. It served me well under our last King, may it do the like for you.

D'ART. I'm honored, father. Thank you. *(d'Art. puts on the sword and belt.)*

MOTHER *(Privately to father)*. Come now. Be strong for your son.

FATHER. Yes. *(Busies himself with d'Art.'s bags.)*

D'ART *(Turning to mother and embracing her)*. Mother.

MOM *(Privately, so Father doesn't hear)*. Come now. Be strong for your father.

D'ART. Yes. *(She kisses him and steps back to let the men say goodbye.)*

FATHER. *(Handing him his bags.)* Goodbye, son. God be with you.

D'ART. Father. *(Going to exit.)*

FATHER. d'Artagnan! Suffer nothing from any man. Fight at every opportunity - all the more willingly because duels are forbidden, hence it takes twice as much courage to fight one.

D'ART. That, father, I promise you. *(They exit.)*

Scene 2

(An Inn on the road to Paris. Hostess enters chasing out Planchet. Two guards are present.)

HOSTESS *(A crash offstage)*. Out! get out of here before I have you arrested!

PLANCHET. But, Madame, you haven't paid me my wages yet.

HOSTESS. You haven't done any work yet! OUT!!

ROCHE *(Entering)*. Any sign of her carriage?

GUARD 1. No, my lord.

ROCHE. Have the orders come?

GUARD 1. Not yet, Monsieur.

ROCHE *(To host)*. Wine. Pray, tell me, you jackals, what could you possibly have found amusing in this appalling . . . hamlet?

GUARD 2. Sorry, sir - nag and rider - coming this way.

(d'Artagnan enters. Planchet notices D'art. The men keep talking, ignoring d'Art.)

GUARD 1. Why, I've got more hair than that horse does.

GUARD 2. It doesn't have a tail.

D'ART *(Passing the men, suspicious)*. Gentlemen. *(They ignore him.)*

GUARD 1. That's not a natural color for a horse.

D'ART *(To host)*. Madame. How much are your rooms?

GUARD 2. Maybe he dyed it. *(The men laugh.)*

D'ART *(To host)*. Just a moment. *(To Roche.)* Pardon, me, sir. Excuse me. Excuse me, sir! You, who hide yourself amongst these giggling grisettes, yes, you! Tell me what it is you're laughing at and we will laugh together.

ROCHE *(Pause)*. I am not speaking to you, sir. *(Turns away.)*

D'ART. Were you laughing at me, sir?!

ROCHE. Most assuredly, sir, I was not laughing at you.

D'ART. Very well, then. Good day. *(He turns to walk away.)*

ROCHE. I was laughing at your horse.

D'ART *(Stopping)*. A man may laugh at a horse, who would not dare to laugh at its master.

ROCHE. I do not laugh often, sir, as you may have perceived from my countenance, nevertheless, I reserve the privilege to laugh whenever I please.

D'ART. And I will not permit any man to laugh when it displeases me.

ROCHE. Indeed, sir. Then it strikes me that you will have a rather lively time of it on your journeys. *(All laugh. Roche. turns away.)*

D'ART *(Drawing)*. Turn! Turn, Master Joker . . . Jester Master, lest I strike you from behind!

ROCHE. Run along, boy. A plague upon these arrogant *Gascons*. *(d'Artagnan lunges, Rochefort avoids.)* Very well.

(Roche. Draws and begrudgingly salutes. As he does, the two other men fall upon D'art. Roche ignores the fight and watches for Milady.)

ROCHE *(During the beating, casually)*. Don't kill him, please. Thank you *(d'Art. Lunges again.)* Unless, of course, our little hero insists upon it. *(To d'Art.)* Be so kind, sir, as to tell us when you have had enough. *(Roche. takes d'Artagnan's sword.)*

D'ART. My sword! I'll take this matter straight to the King! *(A blow knocks d'Art. out.)*

ROCHE. Yes . . . yes, no doubt we've a prince of the blood in disguise. *(To his men of d'Art.)* Search him.

JUSSAC *(Having entered).* My lord. *(Handing Roche. a letter.)* From his Eminence.

HOSTESS. *(Of d'Artagnan.)* I apologize for this, sir. I never saw the gentlemen before.

GUARD 1 *(Having searched d'Art).* Twelve crowns.

GUARD 2 *(Holding up d'Art's mother's jar of ointment).* And this?

GUARD 1. And a letter . . . to the *Captain of the Royal Musketeers, Monsieur Treville!*

ROCHE. The devil! Give me that! If Treville knows we're meeting here . . . Saddle my horse!

GUARD 1 *(Of d'Artagnan).* What about him?

ROCHE. Leave him. *(They all start to exit.)*

MILADY *(Entering with deWardes).* Going somewhere, gentlemen?

ROCHE *(Ushering aside).* Milady - quickly. Monsieur deWardes.

MILADY. Apparently I've missed a little excitement.

ROCHE. It's possible Treville knows of our designs.

MILADY *(Livid).* How?

ROCHE. I'm not sure.

MILADY. Have you the Cardinal's orders?

ROCHE. You are to return to England with all speed and apprise him the moment the Duke of Buckingham leaves London.

MILADY. And you?

ROCHE. I return to Paris.

D'ART *(Coming to. Groggy).* Not before I chastise you, you cowardly wretch!

ROCHE. I hate Gascons.

MILADY *(Seeing Roche. go for his sword)*. Consider, my lord; the slightest delay may ruin everything.

ROCHE. Very well. *(They both exit.)*

D'ART *(Stumbling after him)*. Running away! Turn and fight, you coward! You - *(Falls, still half dazed.)* . . . stand and fight . . . you - why don't you fight!

HOSTESS *(Helping d'Art)*. Sir.

D'ART. Did you see that coward?

HOSTESS. Yes, sir, I did.

D'ART. Did you see?! I challenged him, and he ran!

HOSTESS *(Helping d'Art)*. Indeed, sir, he is a base coward.

D'ART *(Dizzy)*. Yes, base . . . very base . . . but . . . she . . . she was beautiful. *(Faints.)*

(d'Art. is helped off. This exit is overlapped by the entrance of the next scene, as is true with most scenes.)

Scene 3

(The courtyard of Monsieur Treville. Two lines of Musketeers burst on the stage; one retreating, the other advancing in military sword drills. Treville screams out commands. 'En garde! Avancez! Battrez en retraite! Retenez! Cessez! People swarm across the stage: petitioners, people bringing messages, Musketeers waiting for an audience. Others talk and mill about, ducking passing swords and duelists with ease as they continue their conversations. d'Art enters, making his way through, taking everything in. Swordsmen are engaged in a fighting game on the stairs; others are waiting to play. Aramis is reading a bible, at some point a letter is

delivered to him. He reads it, concealing it in the bible. Musketeers make it hard for d'art. to get through, testing him. Planchet is now following d'Artagnan. He waits for d'Artagnan on the periphery.)

MUSK 1 *(To D'ART. Musk 1 is fighting Musk 2).* Out of the way, lack-brain!

D'ART. Excuse me.

MUSK 2 *(To d'Art).* Not that way!

D'ART. Sorry. Excuse me.

MUSK 3 *(Spars with a recruit).* En garde!

D'ART *(Backing into Aramis who is sitting and reading).* Sorry. *(To a Musk.)* Excuse me, do you know where can I find Monsieur Treville? *(Musk. points to his quarters.)*

MUSK 3 *(Giving up on the recruit).* He parries like a woman! *(Musk. #4 takes #3's place.)*

(Porthos has entered, just off guard duty. Under some of the previous dialogue, he exchanges his ceremonial sword with another Musketeer who then takes over guard duty. He puts his own sword on. Porthos is fantastically dressed, in contrast to the others Musketeers. Instead of the uniform cloak, he is wearing a blue doublet with a magnificent golden baldrick over it, and a crimson velvet cloak. He is talking to a few musketeers of his baldrick and affecting a cough.)

PORTHOS. Yes, it is extravagant. But what of that, it's the fashion now.

MUSK 4 *(To the recruit).* Again! *(They fight.)*

MUSK 5 *(Gesturing to Porthos' cloak).* And this?

PORTHOS. Oh, I'm coming down with another cold. *(Feigning a cough.)*

MUSK 3 *(Of Porthos' baldrick)*. I warrant he didn't get that on a Musketeers salary.

MUSK 4 *(Fencing with recruit)*. Don't lurch, you young fool, *lunge*!!

PORTHOS. Upon my faith and honor, I bought it with my own money.

MUSK 1 *(Another conversation somewhere)*. It's obvious: since the Queen spurned his advances, the Cardinal makes for all others.

MUSK 3. He'll never forgive her for that.

MUSK. 1. Yes, our rather potent potentate.

MUSK 2 *(Playing at swords on the stairs)*. A hit! Get down!

MUSK 5. You didn't hit me!

MUSK 3. You're bleeding, fool!

MUSK 5 *(Begrudingly giving up his spot)*. Oh. Very well.

MUSK 1 *(The other conversation)*. Madame Vitrois? She, *too*, said no.

MUSK 3. Poor Cardinal Richelieu should stick to churching and leave the wenching to us.

D'ART *(Trying to break in to a conversation)*. Excuse me.

MUSK 6 *(Running in and announcing)*. I've a duel at noon! Who'll be my second!??

ALL *(Every Musketeer responds immediately)*. I WILL! *(Musk. 6 picks a second.)*

MUSK 4 *(To d'Art)*. What are you doing here and what do you want?

D'ART. Sir. I am here to seek an audience with Monsieur Treville.

MUSK 4. Yes.

D'ART. The Captain of the King's Royal Musketeers.

MUSK 4 . I'm aware of his position. What is yours?

D'ART. Oh, yes - pardon me. I am Monsieur d'Artagnan - a fellow countryman of the Captain. He was - *is* great friends with my father, and he - I'm his protégé - he doesn't know me, but I am quite confident that he'll see me.

MUSK 4. I will convey your request to the Captain.

MUSK 3 *(To recruit, backing him up with sword thrusts).* This may come as quite a surprise to you, but you parry to deflect your enemy's sword not guide it into your own body!! Again!! *(They spar. A cloaked figure delivers a letter to Aramis.)*

PORTHOS *(Entertaining a small crowd around him).* If one cannot live at the expense of their enemy, one must live at the expense of their countrymen. Money must be spent! Don't you agree, Aramis? *(Aramis does not respond.)* He's reading Latin. Shh.

MUSK 3 *(Of the recruit).* I give up! You're not fit for a Musketeer! Send him to the Cardinal!

MUSK 1 *(Reaction from another conversation).* Oh, hang Richelieu *and* his bloody entourage!

MUSK 5. You watch your tongue or you'll find yourself without one.

MUSK 6. Monsieur Chalais lost his head for less.

MUSK 1. What do you think of what his valet says?

PORTHOS. What does he say?

MUSK 2. That he saw Rochefort in Brussels where Chalais was killed.

MUSK 6. Rochefort!

MUSK 3. Cardinal Richelieu's other-self

MUSK 1. Pig.

MUSK 5. Dog.

ARAMIS. Why don't we all just drop the subject.

PORTHOS. Drop the subject! That's all you have to say?

ARAMIS. Well, then let us speak of it, since you desire it so. *(Hides his letters in his bible.)*

PORTHOS. You know, it's a great pity you didn't follow your first vocation - you'd have made a delightful priest.

ARAMIS. And I shall one day. This is merely a temporary postponement.

MUSK 1. Aramis awaits only one thing before resuming the cassock.

PORTHOS. Which, undoubtedly, hangs beneath his uniform.

RECRUIT. And what is it you wait for, Monsieur?

MUSK 1. Only for our Queen to produce an heir to the throne of France.

ARAMIS. It is said the Duke of Buckingham is in France. Perhaps, I shall be a priest sooner than you think. *(This is quite scandalous)*

PORTHOS. Watch your tongue, Aramis!

ARAMIS. Do you propose to teach me how to speak?!

PORTHOS. My dear fellow, either be a priest or a musketeer, but not both at once.

ARAMIS. I will be a priest when it suits me. In the meantime, I am a musketeer, in which quality I say as I please.

PORTHOS. Don't be angry. It's no fault of mine that, though you possess the virtue of discretion when it pertains to your *own* romantic escapades, you lack the ability to employ it with respect to her Majesty.

ARAMIS. I have no idea what you are talking about.

PORTHOS *(Porthos takes Aramis' bible and let's fall the love letters that are in it. Other Musk. laugh).* Oh . . . well then, I assume neither does ~~Madame Aiguillon?~~ Or . . . *(Smelling the letter.)* . . . ~~Madame Bois-Tracy?~~ Or your present mistress, Madame Chevreuse, ~~in Tours,~~ I believe?! *(Aramis leaps at Porthos. They scuffle.)*

MUSKETEERS. Gentlemen! Porthos! Aramis! That will do now!

MUSK 4 *(Yelling out above the din).* Captain Treville will receive Monsieur d'Artagnan! Captain Treville will receive Monsieur d'Artagnan! *(A look from all of "Who?")*

D'ART. *(Extracting himself from the crowd.)* That's me. Excuse me. Pardon. That's me. Yes, I'm d'Artagnan. Your sword, sir - pardon. Thank you.

MUSK 4. This way.

(d'Art. makes his way up stairs. Treville enters, cool and angry, letter in hand, ignoring d'Art.)

TREVILLE. Athos! Porthos! Aramis!!

D'ART *(To Musk. 4 who ignores him).* Shall I wait here? He looks rather busy. Perhaps I should -

TREVILLE *(To Porthos and Aramis).* Presently!!

DART. I'll wait here. Or, if you prefer I could - I'll wait here.

(Aramis and Porthos stand at attention before Treville. d'Art. tries to leave the area but cannot extricate himself. He tries to excuse himself at appropriate moments, but can't.)

TREVILLE. Do you know, gentlemen, what I hear from the King?

ARAMIS. No, Captain, we do not.

PORTHOS. But I should hope, sir, that you will do us the honor to tell us.

TREVILLE. Well, I will do you that honor, sirs. He writes me here, that henceforth he intends to recruit his Musketeers from among the Guardsman of the Cardinal.

ARAMIS. Why would that be, sir?

TREVILLE. Well, I will tell you, sir. It seems that some of the King's Musketeers were involved in a disturbance last night and that the Cardinal's Guards were obliged to take them into custody. Custody!! Arrest the King's Musketeers like some common cloak-snatchers!! And you were among them! Don't try to deny it! The Cardinal himself named all three of you! He - where is Athos?!

ARAMIS. Ill, sir.

TREVILLE. Yes, wounded no doubt! What! *Six* of the Cardinal's Guards arrest *six* of his Majesty's Musketeers!? Only six! *(Porthos attempts to speak.)* Why the Cardinal's men would prefer dying on the spot to being arrested! *(Porthos attempts to speak again.)* To *save* yourselves, to scamper away like frightened schoolboys!   *(To d'Artagnan.)* - WHO ARE YOU!? Who is he?! *(d'Artagnan attempts to speak, Treville continues his previous thought to Aramis and Porthos.)* S'death! - I know what I'll do. I will go straight to the Louvre; I will tender my resignation as captain of the Royal Musketeers and beg a lieutenancy in the Cardinal's Guards! And if he refuses me, zounds! I'll turn monk!

PORTHOS. Captain, the truth is that we *were* six against six - but we were set on quite unawares! And before we had time to draw, two of our party fell dead.

ARAMIS. They did, sir

PORTHOS. And Athos, grievously wounded, was little better.

ARAMIS. So, in actuality, it was six against three.

TREVILLE. He's hurt badly? Athos?

PORTHOS. Very.

ARAMIS. Through the shoulder and into his chest.

PORTHOS. It is to be feared that - *(Athos Enters. Pale. No one dares help him.)*

TREVILLE. Athos!

ATHOS *(Stands at attention with his friends).* You have sent for me, sir. How may I serve my King?

TREVILLE. I was . . . I was just telling these gentlemen . . . that I forbid my Musketeers from needlessly risking their lives! Men of your stamp are few and very dear to the King. *(Athos falls.)* A surgeon! Someone fetch my surgeon! Take him into my study. Quickly! Monsieur Athos, I order you not to die. *(They exit. Treville turns to see d'Artagnan still in the same place.)* You again. What is it you want, boy?

D'ART. My name, sir, is d'Artagnan. I am a Gascon, and it is my intention to -

TREVILLE. d'Artagnan?

D'ART. Yes, Monsieur. My father served with you under -

TREVILLE. Monsieur d'Artagnan. Of Bearn?

D'ART. Yes, sir.

TREVILLE. Pardon me, my dear fellow, I didn't know. Yes . . . yes, I see it now. I loved your father very much. What can I do for his son?

D'ART *(Awkwardly).* Captain, on quitting our home town and coming to Paris, it was my intention to request of you the uniform of a musketeer. I had a letter of introduction but it was stolen from me . . . along with my sword.

TREVILLE. It would make little difference my boy. No one becomes a Musketeer without the experience of several campaigns. But, on account of my old friendship with your father, I will do something for you. I will write a letter to the Royal Academy of Arms and tomorrow you will be admitted - no expense to yourself. Please do not refuse this small service. The best born and richest sometimes solicit it without success. My house will always be open to you.

D'ART (*d'Art. sees Rochefort afar off*). There he is! It's him! That's him! You won't escape me this time! (*Running out.*)

TREVILLE. Who?

D'ART. He! He, the - HIM! The letter thief! Someone stop that man! (*Draws his sword, which is broken in half from previous fight.*) Stop him! Thief! Traitor!

(*d'Art. runs after the man. Treville retires. As d'Art. is bolting down the stairs, Athos is entering. His wound is newly dressed. d'Art. accidentally slams into him.*)

D'ART (*Slams into Athos. Athos lets out a howl*). Excuse me. Excuse me, I'm very sorry, but I'm in a great hurry. (*D. starts away. Athos grabs him.*)

ATHOS. And you regard that as reason enough to cudgel a man?

D'ART. By my faith, it was not intentional and I said, "Excuse me!" I should think that is apology enough. (*Starts away.*)

ATHOS. You are not very polite, are you, boy? A *foreigner*, I assume. (*D. Stops.*)

D'ART *(Walking back to Athos)*. I may not be a native of Paris, Monsieur, but be assured - be *warned*, you are not the man to give me a lesson in good manners. *(Starts off.)*

ATHOS. Monsieur Man-in-a-Hurry, *I* can be found without a chase. Do you understand my meaning?

D'ART. Very well. *(Starts to leave and stops.)* Where, I pray you?

ATHOS. Behind the Luxemburg.

D'ART *(Starts to leave and stops)*. At what time?

ATHOS. Noon.

D'ART. Noon it is.

ATHOS. Try not to keep me waiting, for I should like to have your ears cut off by a quarter past.

D'ART *(Starting away)*. Very well, I'll be there at ten to!

(Athos is helped off, or exits by himself. D. runs across the stage. Porthos enters, showing off his golden baldrick to Musk's 1,2 and 5. As he spreads his cape out to give the men a good look, d'Art. runs into the cape and is enveloped in it. As he struggles to get out of it, Porthos' cape falls off and his golden baldrick is revealed to be a fraud, being made mostly leather.)

PORTHOS. Thunder and hell! *(D. tries to untangle himself.)* What do you think you're doing?!

D'ART. Excuse me, sir, but I'm in a hurry. I'm caught on your sword belt. *(Trying to free himself. When he does, the cape either falls off, or d'Art. maneuvers it in such a way that Porthos' baldrick is revealed.)* Could you - ? Could you help?

MUSK 6 *(The men laugh)*. Oh, ho . . . so this is the new fashion, is it, Monsieur Porthos?

PORTHOS. What?

MUSK 6. What? *(Pointing to Baldrick.)* That!

D'ART. I'm still caught here. If someone could just -

MUSK 4 *(Pointing out the back of Porthos' baldrick).* It's a fake! It's not gold at all!

MUSK 6. It *is* a fake, the back of it's only leather!

PORTHOS *(To D).* Would you . . . .please . . . *(Wrenching him free.)* . . . get off of me!

D'ART. Excuse me. I'm truly sorry, sir, but I'm in a great hurry. I'm chasing someone, and -

PORTHOS. You stand a very good chance of being whipped, my young pup.

D'ART. That's rather presumptuous of you, isn't it?

PORTHOS. Not to a man who's accustomed to looking his enemies in the face.

D'ART. That's true, for I well believe you wouldn't show them your back. *(Walks away. Porthos, enraged, makes after d'Art. and half draws his sword.)* Presently, presently, when you're not wearing your cloak.

PORTHOS. At one o'clock, then.

D'ART. Where?

PORTHOS. Behind the Luxembourg.

D'ART. Very well. One o'clock. *(d'Art. exits.)*

ARAMIS *(Entering).* What's going on here, my friend?

PORTHOS. Nothing.

ARAMIS. Let me help you with your cloak.

PORTHOS. Leave me be, Aramis, would you! *(Storms off.)*

ARAMIS. He must be hungry. *(Aramis continues talking with his followers.)*

D'ART *(Running back onto the stage).* Damn! He's escaped me again, the coward! *(Seeing Aramis.)* Oh, pardon me, Monsieur but you dropped something. *(d'Art. attempts to pick up a richly embroidered, woman's handkerchief that Aramis has dropped. Aramis steps on it. After a brief effort to detain it, Aramis relents.)* I believe, sir, that this is a handkerchief you would be sorry to lose.

MUSK 5. Ah! Now will you persist in saying, my most discreet Aramis, that you are not on *intimate* terms with Madame Chevreuse, when that gracious lady is intimate enough to lend you her handkerchief?

ARAMIS. You are deceived, gentleman; this handkerchief is not mine.

D'ART *(Not realizing his faux pas)*. But, sir, I saw it fall from your -

ARAMIS. You are mistaken. I never saw this handkerchief before in my life. *(A look to D.)*

D'ART *(Realizing his fax pas)*. Well, I didn't actually *see* the handkerchief *fall* from his pocket. It was only near his foot, and so I assumed it was his.

ARAMIS. And you were deceived, my dear sir. *(To Musk 5.)* Besides, this handkerchief might just as well have fallen from your pocket.

MUSK 5. Upon my honor, it did not!

ARAMIS. If you swear upon your honor, and I upon mine, it is quite evident that one of us is lying; and you know where that will lead, don't you? Here, my friend, we will do better than that, let us each take a half. *(He cuts or tears the handkerchief in two, breaking the tension of the moment. The others laugh.)*

MUSK 1. Perfectly fair, I say.

MUSK 2. The judgment of Solomon.

MUSK 5. Aramis, you are indeed full of wisdom - of a kind. *(They shake hands and the men go off in good humor.)*

ARAMIS. Gentlemen. *(Starts off without even looking at D.)*

D'ART. Monsieur, you will accept my apology, I hope.

ARAMIS. Monsieur you will accept my observation, I hope, that you have not acted in this affair as a gentleman should.

D'ART. What!? Do you suppose for a moment that I intended to -

ARAMIS. I suppose, sir, that you are not a fool, and, despite the fact that you come from Gascony, you know very well that people do not stand upon handkerchiefs without good reason. Why were you so asinine as to offer it to me?

D'ART. Why were you so asinine as to drop it?

ARAMIS. I have said, Monsieur, and I will say again, the handkerchief did not fall from my pocket.

D'ART. And in saying so you will have lied about it twice, for I saw it fall.

ARAMIS. If you continue in your present tone I shall have to teach you a lesson.

D'ART. And I shall have to send you back to the pulpit, Monsieur Priest-to-be. Draw, if you please.

ARAMIS. No! No, not here.

D'ART. Ha! Coward.

ARAMIS. Don't worry, my friend, I intend to kill you, depend upon that, but I shall do so in a remote locale where you won't be able to brag about your death to anybody.

D'ART. Behind the Luxemburg?

ARAMIS. Indeed. Shall we say one o'clock, then?

D'ART. Better make it two.

ARAMIS. Very well. Monsieur.

D'ART. Sir. *(Aramis exits.)* Well…if I am fated to be slain today, at least it will be by a Musketeer! *(To Planchet.)* Well, come on. *(They exit.)*

Scene 4

(A barren field behind the Luxemburg. Athos enters, followed by Musk 2.)

MUSK 2. I beg you, sir, listen to reason. You have lost far too much blood to be on your feet and -
ATHOS. There's a great likelihood you might lose some blood of your own if you don't stop pestering me.
MUSK 2. I assure you, sir, Monsieur Treville will be most unhappy if you were to die.
ATHOS *(Drawing his sword)*. Sir, I have a most pressing engagement that I must attend to. *(The noon bell strikes.)* Thank you for the concern, but I am no longer in need of your services. *(Musk 2 exits. Athos sits and waits for D'art. Above and/or behind Athos we see d'Art. bolt across the stage, lost.)*
MUSK 2 *(Stopping on his way out and turning to Athos)*. Monsieur, might I -
ATHOS. Go away, sir.

(Musk 2 continues out. Athos hears, then sees d'Art., but offers no assistance. Not seeing Athos, d'Art. runs off stage, then re-enters meeting Musk 2 who is on his way out.)

D'ART *(Pleading for directions)*. The Luxemburg, sir! Please, I seem to have - there's a gentleman I am to meet, and I - *(Seeing Athos.)* - oh! there he is! *(Waving frantically to him.)* Monsieur! Monsieur Athos!! It's me! *(To Musk 2.)* That's him! Thank you. *(d'Art. runs on stage.)* Monsieur Athos! *(Athos walks to meet d'Art. and politely bows. d'Art responds with a sweeping bow.)* I hope I'm not late. I had to . . . I had to purchase a sword. You see? I think it'll do. I'm not late, am I?

ATHOS. My young sir, you are, indeed, punctual. I have engaged two of my friends as seconds but they are not yet come.

D'ART. I have no seconds on my part, sir. Having just arrived in Paris, I, as yet, know no one but Monsieur Treville.

ATHOS *(Wincing in pain)*. S'death! How you hurt me.

D'ART. If you would permit me, sir - *(Taking out his jar of salve.)* - I have a marvelous ointment for wounds given to me by my mother. In less than three days, I am sure, it will cure you. It would still be a great honor to fight with you then.

ATHOS. I thank you, sir; but I wouldn't dream of having you contemplate your death for three long days.

D'ART. Well, if it be your will to dispatch me at once, please don't inconvenience yourself - *(He goes en garde.)* I'm ready.

ATHOS *(Not moving)*. We will wait for these gentlemen. It will be more correct. Ah! I believe I see one of them now.

D'ART. What! Is Monsieur Porthos your second?

ATHOS. Yes. Any objection?

D'ART. Oh, no, not at all. *(Aramis enters.)*

ATHOS. And here comes the other.

D'ART. And . . . Monsieur Aramis is your other second?

ATHOS. Yes. If you're alive later I'll introduce you.

PORTHOS. And what do you mean by this, Athos!?

ATHOS. Why, this is the gentleman I am going to fight with.

PORTHOS. But *I'm* going to fight with him.

D'ART. But not before one o'clock.

ARAMIS *(Having entered)*. I'm fighting with him also.

D'ART. Yes, but not till two.

ARAMIS *(To Athos)*. What are you two fighting about?

ATHOS. He hurt my shoulder. You?

D'ART. We had a disagreement about fashion.

ATHOS. And you, Aramis?

ARAMIS. Oh, ours is a theological dispute.

ATHOS. Indeed?

D'ART. Yes.

ATHOS. I see.

D'ART. And now we are all here, gentlemen, allow me to offer my sincere apologies.

PORTHOS *(Thinking that d'Art. is trying to get out of the duel. Overlapping)*. Just what I expected.

ATHOS. I should have known.

ARAMIS. You disappoint me.

D'ART. Gentlemen, you misunderstand. I'm apologizing only because there is a great possibility that I will not be able to discharge my debt to all three of you; for Monsieur Athos has the right to kill me first. And now, gentlemen, accepting my apologies - but on this account only - out swords, and - ON GUARD! *(He draws.)*

ATHOS. Well, then, let us begin -

(Just as the fight begins, five of the Cardinals Guards enter. They are Guards #1 and #2, Jussac, Bicarat, and Cahusac.)

ARAMIS. The Guards! The Cardinals Guards!

PORTHOS. Put up! Put up!

ARAMIS. Gentlemen, sheathe your swords!

JUSSAC *(Advancing with his men close behind).* This couldn't be Musketeers fighting again, could it? I have grave doubts about your ability to read, but surely you must have at least *heard* of the edicts against dueling?

ARAMIS. Monsieur Jussac, this is merely a brief fencing lesson for the benefit our dear friend the novice there. Kindly leave us alone.

JUSSAC. Gentlemen, it is with great regret that I must inform you that is impossible. Give up your swords, then, and follow us.

PORTHOS. Pass on your way, sirs, it is the best thing you can do.

JUSSAC. If you disobey we will charge you.

ARAMIS *(To Jussac).* A moment, Monsieur. *(To Porthos and Athos.)* There are five of them, and we are but three.

ATHOS. If we lose, we die here, for, on my part, I swear I will never stand again before the Captain a beaten man. Agreed?

ARAMIS AND PORTHOS. Agreed. *(Both parties prepare to fight.)*

D'ART. Gentlemen, you said there were but three, it appears to me we are four.

PORTHOS. You're not one of us.

D'ART. I've no uniform, but I've the heart of a Musketeer.

JUSSAC. Withdraw, young man, we allow you to do so.

ATHOS. Take his advice, my friend.

D'ART. Try me gentlemen, I swear to you on my honor that I will not leave this field if we are conquered.

ATHOS. What is your name, my brave fellow?

D'ART. d'Artagnan.

ATHOS. Well then, Porthos, Aramis, and *d'Artagnan* . . . forward.

JUSSAC. Have you made up your minds yet, gentlemen?

ARAMIS. We have.

JUSSAC. And what do you intend to do?

ARAMIS *(Drawing swords)*. We are about to have the pleasure of charging you, sir.

JUSSAC. So, you mean to resist?

ARAMIS. I think you could safely say that.

(At the end of Aramis' line, the Musketeers and d'Art. rush the Guards. Athos fights Cahusac, Porthos takes Bicarat, Aramis takes on two unnamed Guards, and d'Art. takes on Jussac. Jussac is a fine swordsman, but d'Art., furious and unorthodox, breaking every rule, makes Jussac lose his patience, and d'Art. eventually runs him through. Aramis quickly dispatches one of his opponents and continues with the other. Bicarat and Porthos wound each other, neither serious and they fight on; Porthos making wise cracks throughout.)

PORTHOS *(To Bicarat as they fight)*. Who makes your doublets, by the way?

(Athos is wounded by Cahusac. He holds his ground but is visibly weakening and in trouble. d'Art., leaps in and takes on Cahusac.)

D'ART *(To Cahusac).* On your guard, sir!

(As soon as Cahusac engages with d'Art. Athos falls to one knee.)

PORTHOS *(To Bicarat as they fight).* What's o'clock, ~~my dear fellow~~? I'm hungry.
ATHOS *(To d'Art. as he presses Cahusac).* S'death! Don't kill him, young fellow! I have an old grudge to settle! Just disarm him - make sure of his - *(d'Art. disarms Cahusac.)* - sword. Well done.

(Cahusac and d'Art. rush for the sword. d'Art. arrives first and steps on it. Cahusac takes a sword from the Guardsmen that Aramis has wounded. On his way back to engage again with d'Art., Athos intercepts him and continues the fight.)

ATHOS *(To d'Art. as he engages Cahusac).* I'm feeling better, thank you. Actually, I'm afraid you might kill him. You're very good.
D'ART. Thank you.

(Aramis now has his sword to the breast of his opponent and is compelling him to sue for mercy. Porthos has been fighting throughout with Bicarat. Athos soon dispatches Cahusac. Everyone is done fighting except Bicarat and Porthos. Aramis, d'Art. and Athos surround the fighters.)

31

PORTHOS *(To Bicarat as they fight).* Getting rather quiet around here, isn't it?

JUSSAC. Bicarat! Yield yourself, you are outnumbered.

BICARAT. I will not yield, sir, but to this spot of earth!

JUSSAC. It is four to one! Leave off, I command you!

BICARAT *(Stops fighting instantly).* Well, if you command me, that's another thing. Duty above all. *(He tosses away his sword.)*

ATHOS *(To Bicarat).* Bravery, sir, is always respected, even in an enemy.

(The three Musketeers and d'Art. all salute Bicarat with their swords and then sheathe them. Then they help Bicarat carry/help off the wounded Guards.)

D'ART *(To the Musketeers).* I may not be a Musketeer yet, but I think it's safe to say I've begun my apprenticeship, have I not?

ATHOS. Indeed you have.

(They all exit.)

Scene 5

(A room in the Louvre. Enter the King speaking to Treville, with Chesnaye, and others in attendance.)

KING. You say, then, the Cardinal's Guards sought out this quarrel with my Musketeers?

TREVILLE. It seems to have fallen out that way, your Majesty.

KING. Hm. His Eminence relates quite a different story. My edicts, I see, go unheeded to the ears of a Musketeer

TREVILLE. What are the men to do, Sire? The Cardinals Guards are forever seeking out quarrels with them, and if only for the honor of the corps, these poor young men are obliged to defend themselves.

KING. Listen to Monsieur Treville! *(Feigning anger.)* You'd think he was speaking of a regiment of monks! *(Privately.)* Is it true my Musketeers were outnumbered?

TREVILLE. Yes, your majesty.

KING. But they were not alone - they had a youth with them?

TREVILLE. Yes, sire, so that three of the King's Musketeers - and this boy - not only maintained their ground against five of the Cardinal's Guards, but ultimately brought four of them to the earth.

KING. Why, this is a victory! A complete victory! *(Catching himself, the King publicly feigns a reprimand to Treville.)* Ah, ah! You incline me to think so! There is no doubt they went there to fight themselves! *(Privately again.)* No wonder the Cardinal was furious. This is good, Treville, this is very good - *(Publicly.)* - very good . . . thing . . . that I don't have the whole company arrested! *(Privately.)* Who is this youth that fought with your men?

TREVILLE. His name is d'Artagnan, sire

KING. I should like to see this young man. No; bring me all four together. I should like to thank them.

TREVILLE. Indeed, you majesty.

KING. But . . . by the back stairs, Treville, by the back; no need to let the Cardinal know.

TREVILLE. Pardon me, your majesty, but the men are presently without.

KING. You brought them here!? *(Calling to his valet.)* Chesnaye! *(To the others.)* Everyone out! Out! I wish to be alone with Monsieur Treville. *(To Chesnaye.)* Show the gentlemen in. *(Mildly rebuking Treville.)* If the Cardinal were to see them I'd never hear the end of it. He doesn't leave me a moments repose at it is. He's perpetually talking to me about Spain, and Austria, and . . .

TREVILLE. England.

KING. England. And the Queen . . . always the Queen. Oh, Treville, I am a most unfortunate King.

TREVILLE. What of the Queen, your majesty?

KING. Oh, things are . . . intimated.

TREVILLE. By whom?

KING. Why who else but he who watches while I sleep, who labors while I amuse myself, who conducts everything at home and abroad, in France and Europe -

TREVILLE. Your majesty is doubtless speaking of God. For I know no one so far above your majesty.

KING. I mean, sir, the prop of my state - I mean the Cardinal.

TREVILLE. His Eminence is not his Holiness, sire.

KING. What do you mean by that, Monsieur?

TREVILLE. I mean only that Papal infallibility does not extend to Cardinals

KING *(Chesnaye enters with the four men)*. Come in! Come in, my heroes. I am going to scold you. *(The three Musketeers advance, bow, d'Art. following close behind. The King feigns a reprimand.)* What the devil, five of his Eminence's guards disabled in two days! That's too many, gentlemen, too many! One or two now and then, I don't say much about, but I'll have to enforce the edicts against dueling if you keep this up.

TREVILLE. Therefore, sire, you see they have come here, repentant, to offer their apologies.

KING. Repentant! I don't trust these hypocritical faces - especially that one yonder with the Gascon look. Come hither, Monsieur. *(d'Art. advances.)*

ATHOS. Pardon me, sire, may I take the liberty to say that had not Monsieur d'Artagnan rescued me, I should not now have the honor of being before your majesty.

KING. Why this Gascon is a very devil! *Ventre-saint-gris!* Monsieur Treville, as the King my father would have said, *Ventre-saint-gris!* Such loyalty must be rewarded. Chesnaye. *(He gives the King a purse.)* The poor Cardinal, five of his best men in two days - but that's enough, gentlemen, please understand, that's enough.

TREVILLE. If your majesty is satisfied, so are we.

KING. Oh, yes I am, Treville. *(Giving d'Art. the money.)* Here's proof of my satisfaction. Thank you for your devotedness, gentlemen. I may continue to rely on it, may I not?

D'ART. We would allow ourselves to be cut to pieces in your majesty's service!

KING. Yes, very well - but keep whole. That will be better for you and more useful to me.

(Treville signals the men to leave. They all four give a sweeping bow to the King and exit.)

KING. Treville, place this young man in the company of the Royal Guards. It will infuriate the Cardinal.

TREVILLE *(Bowing deep and exiting).* Your majesty.

KING.   Chesnaye. Bring me ink and paper and summon my carriage.   I think I shall call upon his Eminence to inquire after the health of poor Jussac. I shall so enjoy the face he's sure to make.

(They exit.)

Scene 6

(Milady enters across the stage, dressed for travel. Kitty is carrying some of Milady's bags. de Wardes also carries some of her things.)

WARDES. I merely suggested that I *accompany* you. I so rarely get to travel these days - especially to England. You could introduce me at the court - that is where you're going isn't it? To London? To the court, yes? Oh, come, Madame, you can confide in me.

MILADY. Kitty, have the coach brought around.

WARDES. You know I can be discreet, Madame, I've proven that, haven't I? And my loyalty to you, and the Cardinal, is beyond question. Take me with you, Madame. I can be a great assistance to you.

MILADY. My lord de Wardes, your assistance is in indeed appreciated in certain areas - this, however, is not one of them. I will contact you when I return.

WARDES. But when? How long till you return? Where will you be in England? You tell me nothing!

MILADY *(Moving in on him)*. Monsieur, you are indeed confection enough for any woman's palette . . . and you are kind . . . and loyal . . . and loving - oh, yes, loving

. . . and discreet - *and meddlesome.* Do not question me of my affairs again. Is that understood?

WARDES. Yes, Madame. *(Gathers up some of her things.)*

MILADY. Good. See me to the carriage . . . and watch the dresses.

(They exit together.)

Scene 7

(About a month later. The common room of the Inn where d'Artagnan is living. Porthos and d'Artagnan are fencing. d'Art. is now in the uniform of the Royal Guards. On stage are Aramis, Athos, and M. Bonacieux. Aramis is writing in a book, and adding up receipts.)

BONA. Gentlemen! Gentlemen, please! I have asked you time and again. Please!

PORTHOS. Oh, do stop jabbering little man.

BONA. Please! *(To Aramis.)* My good sir, I appeal to your gentle nature, if you could only - *(Aramis gently draws his sword and levels it at Bonacieux.)* - would you like some more wine?

PORTHOS *(To d'Art. who is backing up under Porthos attack).* Perhaps you were taught to retreat so in the Guards of Monsieur Dessart, but, I tell you, my boy, a Musketeer would never behave so.

D'ART *(Still retreating).* Monsieur Porthos, may I point out to you that it is not always courage that wins a battle, but often prudence *(Reversing the fight and attacking*

37

Porthos, quite unexpectedly), a knowledge of your opponent's weaknesses . . . learning the established rules . . . and then - breaking them. *(On the words 'breaking them', d'Art. performs a surprising move which leaves his sword point at the neck of Porthos. Athos and Aramis have a small laugh.)* But, *(Freeing Porthos)*, of course, you must have learned this yourself in the Musketeers.

PORTHOS. Indeed . . . I was just seeing if you've been paying attention.

D'ART. My dear friend, I assure you, I am a vigilant observer.

ARAMIS. Yes, and of more than you think, Porthos - and of more than you would care to admit, my dear d'Artagnan.

D'ART. Perhaps.

ATHOS *(To d'Art)*. You will make a fine Musketeer one day.

PORTHOS *(Grabbing Planchet)*. ~~Monsieur~~ d'Artagnan, who - or should I say *what* - is this thing ~~which continually haunts our presence?~~ *that's in my goat?*

D'ART. My servant, Planchet - he followed me home.

PORTHOS. You have a servant?

PLANCHET. Yes, Monsieur, allow me to - *(Porthos shoves Planchet away.)*

PORTHOS. A servant?! And how do you intend to pay ~~him?~~ *her*

D'ART. With the promise of future success.

PORTHOS. Oh. Well, try that on the host and get us another bottle of wine. *(To Planchet.)* YOU! Mongrel! Dog! *(To d'Art.)* That's how you need to speak to servants - yes, YOU! you cabbage-headed cur! - and beat them often. *(To Planchet.)* Stand before me. *(Porthos looks him over.)* Now go away. *(He does.)* He'll do.

ARAMIS. Gentlemen . . . the tally is in. Like all other things of this world which have a beginning and must, one day, have an end, the forty pistoles which the King bestowed upon our young hero, and which was so graciously divided amongst us all, has indeed seen *it's* end.

PORTHOS. What are you sermonizing about now?

ARAMIS. Gentlemen, we're broke.

ATHOS. I'll ask another advance of Monsieur Treville.

ARAMIS. Porthos?

PORTHOS *(Hesitatingly)*. I know a lady friend of mine from whom I believe I can request a small, token, payment for my services . . . *guarding* her - I guard her.

ARAMIS. Indeed. I can sell some theology books. D'Artagnan, have you been paid yet?

D'ART. I'm sorry, no.

ATHOS. Don't apologize, dear fellow, you've provided us with many a meal this past month.

ARAMIS. It is well to sow meals in the days of prosperity so as to reap them in the days of want. If you'll excuse me, now, gentlemen, I'll see what I can reap for us.

ATHOS. Aramis is right. Let us all do the like, and meet at my apartment this evening.

D'ART *(Bonacieux listens closely)*. Begging meals, gambling, fencing lessons, swaggering up and down the streets of Paris - there must be some greater purpose than this that we can aspire to, some nobler way to feed and cloth ourselves! We are four men devoted to each other with both our purses and our lives! Surely, there is nothing we could not accomplish if we but put our hearts to it!

PORTHOS. Let's put our hearts toward acquiring some dinner, the rest will follow in due course. *(They prepare to exit. None of them have money to pay the bill.)*

ATHOS. Come along, my boy. *(To Bonacieux.)* Sir.

ARAMIS *(To Bonacieux).* Sir.

BONA *(To d'Art).* Excuse me, Monsieur.

D'ART. Put it on my bill.

BONA *(To d'Art).* Sir.

D'ART. I told you I will pay. *(To Musketeers.)* I assure you, I'd give ten years of my life to exchange this uniform for that of a Musketeer!

BONA. *(Tapping d'Art. on the shoulder).* Monsieur -

D'ART. WHAT!

BONA. Pardon me, sir, but I couldn't help overhearing you and -

D'ART. Were you spying on us?

BONA. No, no! I promise you, sir, it's just that - you see, I have heard Monsieur d'Artagnan spoken of as a very brave man, and one of great reputation, and -

D'ART. Yes, yes, go on. What are you at?

BONA. Yes, sir, pardon me - I therefore . . . I presume to confide a secret to you, sir.

D'ART *(To the Musketeers).* A moment, gentlemen. *(To Bona.)* Go on, I attend you.

BONA. My wife, sir, is seamstress to the Queen, and, I dare to say - a confident of her majesty. Well, sir, my wife, yesterday morning, was abducted as she was leaving the Queens apartments.

D'ART. The devil!

BONA. And, let me say right away, that I believe love has nothing to do with it. This is somehow connected to the amours of a much greater lady than she.

D'ART. Some nobleman's wife, I suppose?

BONA. Higher, Monsieur.

D'ART. Madame Aigullion, or Madame Chevreuse?

BONA. Higher still, much higher.

D'ART. Of the Queen?!

BONA *(Softly)*. Yes, Monsieur.

D'ART. But with whom?

BONA. The Duke of Buckingham, Monsieur, the Duke of Buckingham. I know it from my wife herself.

D'ART. But why your wife's abduction? *(Bona. hesitates.)* If you wish my help you must give me your complete confidence.

PORTHOS. *(To Bonacieux, having overheard.)* Give him your confidence so we can eat!

ARAMIS. *(To Porthos.)* Have you no discretion, Porthos?

PORTHOS. *(To Aramis.)* I've never been accused of it.

D'ART. *(Moving a little further away.)* Please, go on.

BONA. My wife came home four days ago - my wife who loves me very much - and confided in me that the Queen was in great fear for her friend, the Duke.

D'ART. Yes? Go on.

BONA. The Queen discovered a plot by the Cardinal to write to the Duke of Buckingham in her name to trick him into seeing her again - in order to catch them - catch the Queen and the Duke, um . . . well, you understand, yes?

D'ART. Yes, yes, I understand - but what's this got to do with your wife?

BONA. Well, I'm sure she knows where they're meeting - the Duke and . . . you know - and I'm afraid they'll force her to tell.

D'ART. And the man who carried her off - do you know him?

BONA. Only that he's some lackey of the Cardinal's, and I know what he looks like: lofty bearing, well dressed, black hair, scar on his cheek -

D'ART. A scar! The devil take him! That's my man!

BONA. He - your man, you say?

D'ART. Where can I find him?

BONA. I don't know, Monsieur.

D'ART. A plague upon him!

BONA *(Hesitating)*. I also received this. *(Taking a letter out.)* It came this morning.

D'ART. *(Reading the letter.)* "Do not seek for your wife. She will be returned when there is no longer occasion for her. If you make a single step to find her, you are ruined and she is lost." Well, that's pretty positive.

BONA. I can offer you fifty pistoles. I am no man of the sword, Monsieur, and I fear the Bastille terribly.

D'ART. Indeed, I have no great fondness for the Bastille either.

BONA. I also thought that since you owe me three months rent - for which I have never complained - you might perhaps agree to -

(Rochefort walks into the Inn. Seeing the Musketeers, he exits again. d'Art. sees him, but the other's don't. d'Art. frantically makes after him. The three Musketeers watch with curiosity.)

D'ART. That's him! There he is! Stop! Stop him! That's the man!

PORTHOS. What's he talking about?

D'ART. My sword! Where's my sword!?

ARAMIS *(Calmly)*. Where you put it down.

D'ART. He won't escape me this time! Where's my-?! *(Planchet hands him his sword.)*

PORTHOS. Where are you off to now? We haven't eaten yet!

D'ART. It's him! It's him again! *(He runs off.)*

PORTHOS. What was he talking about?

ARAMIS. I believe it's that fellow he's been chasing around Paris.

ATHOS. The one who stole his letter.

D'ART *(Enters, running across the stage and continues out the other side)*. I think he went around the back! *(Exits.)*

PORTHOS. He's not had much luck running that fellow down, has he?

ATHOS. Decidedly not.

PORTHOS *(Of a letter Aramis is reading)*. Can I see? *(Aramis slaps his hand away.)* Perhaps you could read it to us?

ARAMIS. Must you continuously talk?

PORTHOS. When I talk I forget I haven't eaten.

(d'Artagnan enters having, once again, lost his man.)

ATHOS. Well?

D'ART. That man is the devil himself! A plague upon him! He's vanished again!

PORTHOS. Can we go now?

D'ART. There's no need to. Monsieur Bonacieux! Three bottles of your best Beaugency. Gentlemen, I believe this devil with the scar may have brought a glorious piece of business to our hands, one that will earn us fifty pistoles and, perhaps, do a great service to the Queen. *(Four Guards enter the Inn.)* I will explain later, suffice it to say we are now in the employ of Monsieur Bonacieux.

(The Guards: Bicarat, Cahusac, Guards #1 and #2, hesitate at the door when they see the Musketeers.)

PORTHOS. What's this?

BONA. Save me, gentlemen! They've come to arrest me! For the love of heaven, save me!

D'ART *(To the Musketeers who have started to draw their swords).* A moment, gentlemen.

ATHOS *(To Aramis and Porthos).* Do as he says, he has the best head of the four of us.

D'ART *(To the officers).* Come in, gentlemen, come in. We are all faithful servants of the King and Monsieur the Cardinal.

GUARD 1. Then, gentlemen, leaving our personal conflicts aside, I assume you will not prevent us from carrying out our orders.

D'ART. On the contrary; we will assist you if necessary. *(Pushing Bona. toward the Officers.)* You're a shabby old fellow, my dear sir! Demanding rent money of me! To prison with him, gentlemen!

BONA. But Monsieur! Monsieur, you promised -

D'ART *(Grabbing Bona again. Outloud).* Hold your tongue, man! *(Privately.)* We cannot save you or your wife if we are arrested too. *(Outloud.)* Take him, gentlemen.

BONA. But, Monsieur! Shall I hear from you!? How will I - ?

D'ART. Take the villain away! and be done with him! *(They drag Bonacieux out.)* That went rather well.

PORTHOS. Now, what the devil was that!? This poor innkeeper begs us for help and we let him be arrested!?

ATHOS. Porthos, I have, on more than one occasion, pointed out to you that you are a fool.

ARAMIS. As have I.

PORTHOS. Then you approve of this action?

ATHOS. I do.

PORTHOS. Well, I'm quite lost.

ARAMIS. You usually are.

D'ART. I will explain all - but not here. Let's retire to my apartment - but, first, gentlemen . . . we are every man for the other, we have sworn, have we not?

ATHOS *(Simultaneously)*. Of course.

ARAMIS *(Simultaneously)*. Yes.

PORTHOS. Well -

ATHOS. Porthos.

PORTHOS *(Grumbling)*. Yes.

D'ART. That's well, because from this moment on, gentlemen, we are at war with the Cardinal.

(They exit in the direction of d'Art.'s apartment. Porthos grabs a few bottles of wine.)

Scene 8

(The Louvre. In the Queens private chambers. Queen Anne, and Dona Estefana attending.)

ANNE *(Letters in her hand)*. I have little time, quickly, has there been any word on Madame Bonacieux?

DONA. No, Madame.

ANNE. And my lord, the Duke of Buckingham? Received he my letter?

DONA. This came this morning, Madame.

ANNE. Make sure no one is listening. *(Dona hands her a letter. She reads.)* He is in France . . . and is well. Good, he knows the letter he received was a forgery, but ". . . regardless, will wait another day at the . . . place we spoke of . . . if your Lady does not appear I will . . . continue on to see you." What folly! *(Handing her the letter.)* Destroy this. I knew he wouldn't turn back. He persists in seeing me, risking his own life and my honor despite my entreaties. I warned him not to come again to France! He knows the Cardinal is laying a trap for him, and yet, still, he comes!

DONA. He would come had he your permission or not, Madame, you know that.

ANNE. Yes. Yes, I do. *(To herself.)* Two fools we. *(Outloud.)* And now my dear Constance has disappeared. How could the Cardinal have known our intents?

DONA. His spies are everywhere Madame. No face can be trusted for what it seems.

ANNE. I refused to see him, did I not? I begged him not to come!

DONA. You did, Madame. Do not blame yourself.

ANNE. Who, then, shall I blame? Everything keeps us apart, the depths of the sea, the enmity of kingdoms, the sanctity of marriage vows; surely it is sacrilege to struggle against such odds.

DONA. Is it not, Madame, also sacrilege to keep apart two hearts which God undoubtedly made for one another?

ANNE. You forget, my dear, the King and I are a marriage of nations, not hearts; indeed, it is a heartless alliance; but an alliance nonetheless, and it demands a sort of . . . sanctity.

(A knock at the chamber. Chesnaye enters.)

CHESNAYE.   Madame, the King requires your attendance.

ANNE. Tell him I come. *(Chesnaye exits.)*

DONA. Shall I go myself in the stead of Madame Bonacieux?

ANNE. Indeed, I have not seen him in quite some time.

DONA. No, Madame.

ANNE. He is a stubborn man.

DONA. He will come whether you will or no.

ANNE. If only to urge him to leave Paris at once.

DONA. Yes, Madame.

ANNE *(Having decided).* No. No. We mustn't see him. He must respect my demands. There is far too much at risk. If he -

CHESNAYE *(Entering again).* Your majesty.

ANNE. We come.

DONA *(Privately).* Shall I go to speak with him, Madame?

ANNE *(Privately to Dona as they exit).* No. It's too dangerous. We shall try another message.

Scene 9

(Bonacieux's Inn. d'Artagnan enters with his servant, Planchet, searching the house.)

PLANCHET. Yes, Monsieur, but you promised me 30 sous a day! Thirty days ago!

D'ART. You'll receive a payment quite sooner than you expect if you don't stop grumbling all the time - look over there. Anything could be helpful, letters, bills of fare - maybe the registry.

PLANCHET. I don't believe my demands to be unreasonable. Good day, Monsieur, I am quitting your service.

D'ART *(Grabbing Planchet)*. Planchet, I forbid you to leave my service without my permission. My future cannot fail to be more prosperous, therefore your fortune is made if you remain with me, and I am too good a master to let you to miss such an opportunity.

PLANCHET. But -

D'ART. Unless you prefer a sound thrashing.

PLANCHET *(Returning to searching the apartment)*. Did you look through here, master?

D'ART. Yes. Try the other side - someone's coming! Planchet! Over here! Quick!

(They conceal themselves. From where d'Art. is, he can't see very clearly. Constance Bonacieux runs in being pursued by two of the Cardinal's men. A quick chase and scuffle around the Inn. After catching her, they are very rough with her.)

D'ART. Stay back, Planchet! See what we can learn!

CONSTANCE. Keep your hands off me! I tell you, I am the mistress of this house!

GUARD 2. We know who you are. Bind her! Hurry!

CONSTANCE. Gentlemen, I beg of you - there's been some mistake. I - OW! Please . . . please . . . don't - *(They tie her hands behind her back and gag her.)*

D'ART. The scoundrels - where's my sword?!

PLANCHET *(Shifting d'Art.'s swordbelt which has twisted around his back).* Here, sir.

D'ART. Good. Planchet, run and seek out my friends. Tell them to come, armed, and be quick about it.

PLANCHET. And where are you going, sir?

D'ART. To the rescue. To rescue the lady, of course.

PLANCHET. Might you not pay me my wages *before* you kill yourself?

D'ART. Be quiet, you fool, and go!

(d'Artagnan engages the two men. One of them isn't armed, so after making an initial defense, with anything he can find, he flees quickly. d'Art. makes quick work of the other, who flees.)

D'ART *(As he engages them).* I see you have quite a way with the women, gentlemen. How are you with a sword? *(After they flee.)* You run well enough! Cowards. *(He quickly attends to Constance who is still bound and gagged, he takes the gag off.)*

CONSTANCE. *(Unsure of his intents.)* I am of the Queen, sir!

D'ART. I mean you no harm, Madame. *(A short beat. Both taken with each other.)*

CONSTANCE. You have saved me. I thank you.

D'ART. You owe me no thanks, Madame. I did as any gentleman would.

CONSTANCE. Could you - ? My hands.

D'ART. What? Oh! Yes . . . *(Untying her hands.)*

CONSTANCE. Thank you. Where is Monsieur Bonacieux?

D'ART. Why, do you know him, Madame?

CONSTANCE. He is my husband.

D'ART. Your . . . your husband?

CONSTANCE. Yes.

D'ART. You're married to that - him - he's your husband?

CONSTANCE. Indeed, sir. Do you know where he is?

D'ART. He was arrested and taken to the Bastille.

CONSTANCE *(Not terribly displeased with this news, but discreet about the fact).* Oh, my God, what has he done?

D'ART. I think his only crime consists of having the good fortune of being your husband.

CONSTANCE. Then you know -

D'ART. I know you were abducted by the same villain I've been searching for myself. Did you happen to learn his name, Madame?

CONSTANCE. No. He never spoke to me.

D'ART. And he released you? Unharmed?

CONSTANCE. No. I took advantage of a brief moment I was left alone. I didn't know where to go, so I ran here, but the Cardinal's guards were waiting for me.

D'ART. And they're sure to return. This is no place for you, Madame. May I escort you somewhere?

CONSTANCE. Yes. Yes, you can. *(Takes him by the arm and ushers him along.)* Quickly, there's no time to lose. *(A beat. Very serious.)* Are you a man to be trusted, Monsieur . . . what is your name?

D'ART. d'Artagnan.

CONSTANCE. Monsieur d'Artagnan, are you a man to be trusted?

D'ART. Upon my word of honor and my faith as a gentleman.

CONSTANCE. Come with me, then.
D'ART. Quickly, someone's coming
CONSTANCE. No, this way!

(They exit. Planchet runs on with the three Musketeers, armed.)

ATHOS. Aramis, look in the back! Porthos, check his apartment! *(To Planchet.)* How many you say?
PLANCHET. There were three of them, Monsieur, and a woman.
ARAMIS. Nothing!
PLANCHET. He's killed himself, surely.
ATHOS. Be quiet.
PLANCHET. There go my wages.
PORTHOS. He's not here.
ATHOS. Did he say anything else?
PLANCHET. No. The lady screamed, he ran to the rescue, and I ran away - under orders!
ATHOS. Very well. Go back to my apartment and stay there.
PLANCHET. I'm no coward, gentlemen, I assure you.
ATHOS. I haven't a doubt.
PLANCHET. I tried to -
PORTHOS. Go away!
PLANCHET. Yes, Monsieur. *(Starts to go.)* Might Monsieur loan me the cost of a meal?
ATHOS. GO!
PORTHOS. Well, what do we do?
ATHOS. I'm thinking.

PORTHOS. I don't know about this business. We may get fifty pistoles out of Bonacieux, but is it worth risking our heads?

ARAMIS. Obviously the honor of a woman is at stake, surely that is reason enough.

ATHOS. Beware, Aramis; all women are not as they seem. Neither is their honor.

PORTHOS. Well, if it means playing the Cardinal a bad turn, I guess I'll take the risk.

ATHOS. As would I.

ARAMIS. And I.

ATHOS. Gentlemen, I believe we have an adventure. Let us begin by finding d'Artagnan. Porthos, return to my apartment and wait for him there. Aramis, see if you can discover if anyone was admitted to the Bastille tonight. I'll to Monsieur Treville.

(They exit.)

Scene 10

(A street in Paris. Enter Constance and d'Artagnan.)

D'ART. Can you not tell me who it is you're going to meet?

CONSTANCE. It is not my secret to tell.

D'ART. Shall I wait for you?

CONSTANCE. No.

D'ART. But where will you go tonight?

CONSTANCE. I have places to go.

D'ART. You intend to make your way there alone?

CONSTANCE. Perhaps I shall, perhaps not.

D'ART. You are the most mysterious woman I have ever met.

CONSTANCE. Do I lose much by that?

D'ART. On the contrary, Madame.

CONSTANCE. Leave me now.

D'ART. I will wait outside the door.

CONSTANCE. I asked for the assistance of a gentleman, not a spy. Honor your word and leave me now.

D'ART. I will, Madame, but I will discover your secrets one day.

CONSTANCE *(Serious)*. Beware of what you say! Let it be as if you had never seen me.

D'ART. If you knew what I was feeling you would know that is impossible.

CONSTANCE. You speak rather suddenly of feelings, Monsieur.

D'ART. That is because they have come upon me so suddenly, Madame.

CONSTANCE. I beg you to leave me now.

D'ART *(Kisses her hand, ardently)*. I wish I had never seen you!

CONSTANCE. Well . . . I cannot say as much to you. What is lost for today may not be lost forever.

D'ART. You are enchanting.

CONSTANCE. Perhaps. Now go.

D'ART. Adieu, Madame, Adieu. *(Begins his exit.)*

(Constance knocks on the door. After a few knocks, the door is opened and she is pulled violently inside. She lets out a scream. The door is slammed shut. d'Art. runs back on.)

D'ART. Madame! Madame Bonacieux! *(Banging on the door. Trying to find a way in.)* Open the door! Madame, can you hear me!?

(As d'Art. moves away from the door in search of a way in. Constance, with a black cloak, now, her hood pulled down, and a man come out of the house. He is dressed as a Musketeer. He holds a handkerchief to his face to help obscure his identity. d'Art. leaps in front of them.)

D'ART. Hold, sir!
BUCK. What do you want, Monsieur?
D'ART. Madame Bonacieux.
CONSTANCE. Monsieur!
BUCK *(To Constance).* Silence! *(to d'Art.)* I gather you have mistaken this woman for someone that you know, and so I pardon you.
D'ART. You pardon me!
CONSTANCE *(To d'Art).* Monsieur, you gave me your word!
D'ART. I heard you scream, Madame! You were dragged into a strange house.
CONSTANCE. That's because I was seen with you!
BUCK. Excuse me. I have an extremely pressing engagement. Perhaps the two of you can discuss this another time. Take my arm, Madame, and let us go.

(Buck. pushes d'Art. aside as he walks by with Constance. d'Art. draws his sword. Instantly, Buck. swings around, drawing his sword also.)

CONSTANCE. In the name of heaven, Your Grace!
D'ART *(Dawning on him who this is).* Your Grace?

CONSTANCE.   His   Grace,   the   Duke   of Buckingham!

D'ART *(Dropping to his knees)*.   Your Grace - a thousand pardons, sir, but I feared for her safety. Forgive me and tell me how I may serve you?

BUCK.   Walk   behind   at   twenty   paces,   if   anyone follows us, kill him. *(They exit.)*

Scene 11

(An investigation room in the Bastille. One table, one chair. Monsieur Bonacieux is lead on by two guards. He is brought before Richelieu who is sitting at a small table reading over papers. An attendant or two are on stage also. Richelieu is not dressed in his Cardinals robes. Bonacieux has never seen the Cardinal, so he doesn't know to whom he is speaking.)

GUARD 1. This way, Monsieur.

BONA.   There's   been   some   terrible   mistake, gentlemen. I'm completely innocent! I don't even know why I'm here!

GUARD 1. Be quiet.

BONA. Oh, God, this is it, yes? This is how it goes? Taken from your cell in the middle of the night and - and - oh, God!   Might   one   of   you   gentlemen   act   as   my confessor? I know it's a somewhat unorthodox request, but you must admit, these are extreme circumstances.

(By the end of this speech, Bonacieux has been tossed in front of Richelieu. Richelieu is looking over paperwork. After an uncomfortable pause he speaks.)

RICHELIEU. Are you Bonacieux?

BONA.   Jacques Michel Bonacieux, fifty-one, Innkeeper, number 16 Rue des Fossoyeurs.

RICHELIEU. I urge you, sir, to reflect deeply on the seriousness of your situation.

BONA. I beg you to believe me. Monsieur, I have done nothing wrong!

RICHELIEU. How comes it, then, that you find yourself in the Bastille accused of high treason.

BONA. Treason! That's impossible, Monsieur, I - I detest the Protestants, I abhor the Spaniards! How could I possibly be a traitor, I hate all the right people!?

RICHELIEU. It says here you have conspired with your wife, with a Monsieur d'Artagnan, and the Duke of Buckingham.

BONA. I swear to you, I have not! I know those names, but I have done nothing!

RICHELIEU. How do you know the name of Buckingham?

BONA. My wife mentioned to me, in passing, that she had heard - from someone whom I don't know - that the Cardinal had seduced the Duke of Buckingham to France in order to compromise him with the Queen.

RICHELIEU. Hold your tongue, you imbecile!

BONA. That's exactly what my wife said.

RICHELIEU. You're wife was abducted. Do you know by whom?

BONA. No, Monsieur.

RICHELIEU. You have suspicions?

BONA. Yes, Monsieur, but my suspicions seemed to have landed me in the Bastille, so I no longer have them.
(A messenger enters.)

GUARD 2. The Count is here and requests to speak to your Eminence immediately.

RICHELIEU. Send him in.

BONA. Your Eminence?!

RICHELIEU *(Gesturing to his attendants who begin to dress him in his Cardinal attire).* You have not, I take it, ever had the opportunity to meet Cardinal Richelieu, have you?

BONA. No, Monsieur, I have never - I - no.

RICHELIEU. Allow me introduce myself.

BONA. Oh, my God!

RICHELIEU. Not exactly. *(Rochefort enters with two guards.)*

BONA. That's him! There he is! That's the man!

RICHELIEU. What man?

BONA. The man who took away my wife!

RICHELIEU. That man is a friend of mine *(The guards grab Bonacieux.)*

BONA. It's *not* him! No, Monsignor, *no,* that's not the man! No, I've made a great mistake! That's quite a different man. *(The guards take him away.)* Doesn't resemble my man at all! This man here, I'm sure is a very respectable person - man - gentleman!

RICHELIEU *(Of Bonacieux).* That head has never conspired to do a thing. *(To Roche.)* How now, Monsieur, what news?

ROCHE. They have seen each other.

RICHELIEU. The Queen and Buckingham!?

ROCHE. Yes. At the Louvre.

RICHELIEU. Who told you of it?

ROCHE. Madame Estefana.

RICHELIEU. How long was the Duke with her?

ROCHE. Perhaps half an hour.

RICHELIEU. Damn her!

ROCHE. Dona Estefana claims that, on parting, they exchanged letters and Her Majesty gave the Duke a rosewood casket.

RICHELIEU. Does she know what was in it?

ROCHE. Yes - the diamonds His Majesty gave the Queen.

RICHELIEU. His Majesty's gift to the Queen . . . *(Ruminating.)* . . . perhaps, then, all is not lost. Good, Rochefort, good. This may even be for the best. *(To one of his attendants.)* Bring the prisoner back in. And send for Jussac. *(To Roche)* If found, do not arrest this d'Artagnan. Let the Queen believe she is perfectly safe. She mustn't think that we know her secret. I'll to the King and give him the news of Buckingham's visit. *(Bonacieux is brought back in.)* Monsieur Jacques Michel Bonacieux . . .

BONA. Yes, your most exalted Holy Eminence.

RICHELIEU. After careful deliberation . . . I find you to be an honest man. Rise, my good friend. *(The Cardinal helps him up.)* Rise. As you have been unjustly suspected, you must be recompensed. Take this purse, pardon me, and be on your way.

BONA. *I* pardon *you*!? I - yes, of course, Your Eminence - but you were quite right to arrest me - if you want to. You may arrest me anytime you like - at your convenience, of course.

RICHELIEU. Yes, yes. Farewell, then, or rather au revoir, for I do hope that we shall see each other again.

BONA. *(Bowing low and backing out of the room.)* Yes, I - well - yes! whenever you wish, Monsignor.

RICHELIEU. I look forward to it. I have enjoyed your company. Forgive me, my friend, but I'm a very busy man. Goodbye for now.

BONA. *(To Guards as he exits.)* He called me his friend. Did you hear that? I'm a friend of the Cardinal. *(He exits, exuberant.)* He likes me.

RICHELIEU. There goes a man who, henceforth, will lay down his life for me.

ROCHE. Do you wish anything else done with this fellow?

RICHELIEU. No. I've done all that can be done with that sort of a man; I've made him a spy upon his own wife. *(Jussac enters with paper and ink.)* Leave me for now.

ROCHE *(Bowing and exiting).* Your Grace.

RICHELIEU *(Gesturing everyone else out also).* The rest, too. *(They all exit.)* Jussac, you will, with all speed, immediately to London and deliver this message to Milady de Winter. *(He nods his head yes. Dictating.)* "The Duke of Buckingham is in possession of a set of twelve diamonds. Attend every ball and affair of state. He is sure to wear them. Get close to him and *cut off two.* Inform me as soon as they are in your possession."

(They exit.)

Scene 12

(Late. An inn. Enter the Three Musketeers, d'Artagnan and Planchet. Athos drunk.)

PORTHOS. You could at least tell us where you've been? We've had half of Paris looking for you!

D'ART. My own secrets I would willingly share, but not those of another. I apologize for any inconvenience I've put you to.

PORTHOS. Oh, no inconvenience. I enjoy being dragged away from my dinner - boots in hand - by this mangy excuse for a servant.

PLANCHET. I resent that, sir. I -

D'ART *(To Planchet).* Hold your tongue!

ARAMIS. Can you tell us anything?

D'ART. I feel - for Madame Bonacieux's safety - we should let the matter rest.

PORTHOS *(Teasing d'Art).* Ah, mystery, intrigue, a woman - you acclimate quickly to life in Paris for a Gascon farmer boy.

ATHOS. Porthos.

PORTHOS. I'm sorry. I'm hungry. I'm irritable when I'm hungry.

ATHOS. Gentlemen, leave us.

PORTHOS. Are we not to eat?

ATHOS. My friend, go away.

ARAMIS. Come along, Porthos.

PORTHOS *(To Athos).* As you wish . . . Monsieur Melancholy.

ARAMIS *(Privately, leading Porthos off).* Enough. Don't anger him.

ATHOS *(To Planchet).* You too. *(Planchet exits. To d'Art.)* Tell me, my young friend, is this Madame Bonacieux . . . a handsome woman?

D'ART. She's beautiful, Athos.

ATHOS. I assumed as much. A piece of advice: in the art of intrigues . . . mistrust the women much more than the men.

D'ART. Not this woman, Athos. She is goodness and beauty itself. An angel.

ATHOS *(A sardonic laugh).* Ha.

D'ART *(Defensive).* I am in love with her, Athos.

ATHOS. Love!? God, how ludicrous.

D'ART. Ludicrous!? And what do you know of love to speak to me so?

ATHOS. Yes, what do I know of love. My apologies. Have a drink.

D'ART. Pardon me, my friend, I cannot drink with you. *(Starts to leave.)*

ATHOS. Son. Stop. I'm sorry. I was only trying to . . . trying to protect you.

D'ART. I'm quite capable, Monsieur, of protecting myself.

ATHOS. Yes . . . I'm sure you are. Please, sit. Sit, and I will relate to you a real story of love. I shall advise through parable.

D'ART. Does this story concern you?

ATHOS. . . . A friend of mine. *(d'Art. sits.)* I shall tell it better if I drink. The two go well together. *(He pours wine.)* One of my friends - an acquaintance of mine, you understand, not myself - one of the Counts of my province, a young man of twenty-five, fell in love with a girl - a beautiful girl, barely eighteen. She worked with a priest, in a small town under the jurisdiction of my friend. This friend, the Lord and Count of the province, was an honorable man and courted her for months, laid gifts at her feet, professed his love, and married her, triple ass that he was!

D'ART. How so if he loved her?

ATHOS. You shall see. One day while out hunting with her husband, she fell from her horse and fainted. The Count ran to help her, and loosening her bodice to let her breathe . . . what do think he saw?

D'ART. What?

ATHOS. A fleur-de-lis. Neatly branded cross her breast.

D'ART. What are you saying?

ATHOS. The truth! She had the scar of the fleur-de-lis burned into her lily-whiteness. All her months of false modesty hid not her shame, but rather the brand of a criminal. The *angel* was a fiend - not the beautiful, naive bride who arrayed herself so stunningly in virginal white - no, she was a *whore* and a *thief.* Oh, yes, and the priest she worked for, well, he turned out to be nothing more than her current lover, and the Count, a gull and an imbecile! This dissembling strumpet . . . this enchantress . . . this *counterfeit* was plotting his death - for *money* . . . .for my estate.

D'ART. My God. And what became of her?

ATHOS. The Count was the lord high magistrate of the land, with the power to execute justice . . . he tore off the rest of her clothes, bound her hands behind her back, and hanged her from a tree - I seem to have no wine - that cured me of love, to be sure. Drink, my friend.

D'ART. I've had more than enough, thank you.

ATHOS. Ah, you young fellows nowadays don't know how to drink. It's a lost art, and one that is very much under appreciated. Wait here, and I'll get some more wine.

D'ART. Come, Athos, it's late. Let me help you to my room.

ATHOS *(Pushing d'Art. away).* I need no help; I need wine. You need the help. *(Exiting.)* This lady friend - let her go . . . love is a lottery, my young fellow, in which he who wins, wins death. May God grant you always lose in that game.

(Exits. He stumbles off. d'Art. follows off to help him.)

Scene 13

(In the Louvre.)

KING *(Yelling)*. Buckingham in Paris!! Why was he here!?

RICHELIEU. I can only guess -

KING. Yes!? What!?

RICHELIEU. To conspire, no doubt, with your enemies, my lord.

KING. Yes, you tell me that - by God, he's come to conspire against my honor!

RICHELIEU. I am quite sure, your Majesty, that Buckingham's sojourn in Paris was purely for political reasons.

KING. And I am quite sure it was purely for another purpose!

RICHELIEU. I cannot think the Queen would be so indiscreet.

KING. Well, I can!

RICHELIEU. However, as much as pains me to even consider a betrayal of the King - and France - such as the one you speak of, your Majesty compels me to think of it; Madame Dona Estefana told me this very morning, she found the Queen weeping inconsolably while writing a letter -

KING. That's it! To *him* no doubt! Writing love letters to the enemies of France!

RICHELIEU. Your Majesty, the Queen is too prudent a -

KING. I'll search everywhere! I'll search her own person if necessary!

RICHELIEU. I beg you to consider, my lord, the Queen is one of the greatest princesses in the world.

KING. She is all the more guilty for that very reason! The more she has abused the exalted position she has been given, the lower she has fallen! I tell you she doesn't love me, but that English . . . that villain Buckingham! Why didn't you have him arrested while he was in Paris!?

RICHELIEU. Arrest the Prime Minister of King Charles I? Think of the scandal, your Majesty. And if your suspicions proved true - which I, of course, still doubt - what a terrible disgrace it would be.

KING. Still you doubt!? She was writing to him, wasn't she?! I'm sure of it. I want those letters! I want them now!

RICHELIEU. Since you will have it so, there is but one means: charge Monsieur Jussac with the matter. It falls well within the duties of his post.

KING. Let him be sent for immediately.

RICHELIEU. Yes, your Majesty - but . . .

KING. Yes? What?

RICHELIEU. The Queen may, perhaps, refuse to obey Jussac if she does not know that the orders came from the King himself.

KING. Well, I will satisfy her doubts fully then - I will tell her myself!

(They exit. The Queen enters elsewhere, talking to Constance, accompanied by Estefana.)

ANNE. Have you heard nothing else, then?

CONSTANCE. No Madame. Only that his Grace is safely out of France.

ANNE. Not in England yet?

CONSTANCE. No Madame.

ANNE. I have another letter.

CONSTANCE. Yes. Shall I take it now?

ANNE. No. I am spied upon by my own women. I am sure of it.

CONSTANCE. I will come to you tonight.

ANNE. Take care, sweet Constance, you must remember to be cautious in all your - *(Seeing the King enter, Anne sends Constance off.)* - quickly!

KING *(Entering)*. Madame, you are about to receive a visit from Monsieur Jussac. He will communicate to you certain matters with which I have charged him.

ANNE. What can Monsieur Jussac have to say to me that your Majesty cannot say yourself? *(The King exits.)* Your Majesty?

JUSSAC *(Bowing)*. Madame.

ANNE. What do you desire of me, sir?

JUSSAC. Without prejudice to the respect due your Majesty I come, in the King's name, to make an inspection of your papers.

ANNE. That's absurd! and a proceeding quite unworthy of you or the King - or should I say the Cardinal!

JUSSAC. I serve the King and the King only, Madame.

ANNE. When it's convenient you do, Monsieur. Examine, then. I am a criminal, it seems. Dona Estefana, give him the keys to my desks and closets.

JUSSAC. That will not be necessary, Madame.

ANNE. What is it you mean, Monsieur?

JUSSAC. You may spare us both embarrassment, Madame, if you would be so gracious as to give over any papers that you may have on your person. *(Anne's hand, impulsively goes to her breast, where the letter is.)* Pray, give me the letter, Madame. I am authorized to search even Your majesty's person.

ANNE. You would dare to lay hands on your Queen!

JUSSAC. I am a faithful subject to the King, Madame.

ANNE. I will not suffer it, Monsieur! I would sooner die!

(Jussac bows and then slowly approaches the Queen. When he is at arms length, he reaches a hand toward out to her. Anne steps back, and takes the letter out.)

ANNE. There, Monsieur! There is the letter. Take it and relieve me of your odious presence. *(Jussac takes the letter and bows. He starts away.)* My ladies, come.

(The Queen exits with her women. Jussac has taken but a few steps when the King, who has been waiting just outside, rushes on. The Cardinal enters with him.)

KING. Give me that, sir. Give it to me. I knew it! *(Turning the letter over in his hands. Opening it. Trembling at first, the King reads that it is not to Buckingham and becomes suddenly very happy.)* Writing sweet nothings to that nothing of a - it's not to him . . . it's - it's to the King of Spain! . . . *(Reads rapidly.)* . . . Dear brother . . . .constant humiliation of the House of Austria . . . at once threaten war against France . . . and -* there's not a word about love in here, Monsieur! Not one word!

Ha, ha! It's only a plan for her brother, the Emperor of Austria, to attack France! Isn't that wonderful! - actually to attack *you* in particular, Monsieur. It seems Spain is quite offended by some of your recent policies. She invites her brother here to threaten war against France and make the one condition for peace your dismissal. How about that! Your dismissal! Not a love letter at all! The whole intrigue is political and there is not the least question of love in this letter. *(Handing the letter to the Cardinal.)* However, there is abundant question about you.

RICHELIEU. Well, your Majesty, you see how far my enemies go. I never should have mentioned that letter.

KING. True, Monsieur, nevertheless the Queen is more than deserving of the King's wrath.

RICHELIEU. Sire, the Queen is a devoted, irreproachable wife. I instigated all of this with my foolish doubts. Allow me then, Monsieur, to intercede with you on her behalf.

KING. Let her come to me and apologize then.

RICHELIEU. I beseech you, sir, to set the example yourself.

KING. Never! She was in the wrong!

RICHELIEU. As were you, sir, for falsely suspecting the Queen.

KING. Ridiculous. *(Changing his tone.)* How might I set such an example if I so wished?

RICHELIEU. By doing something that you know will please her.

KING. I don't know what pleases her.

RICHELIEU. There must be something . . . a gift of some sort . . . she does so love to dance . . . wasn't she asking you to host another ball recently?

KING. Asking? She was tormenting me!

RICHELIEU. That's it, Sire! Let us host a royal ball in her majesty's honor.

KING. You know I don't care in the least for these foolish balls.

RICHELIEU. The Queen will then be all the more grateful to you, sir. Besides, it will be an opportunity for her to wear those beautiful diamonds that you gave her recently. She has had no such occasion to wear them yet.

KING. Well, we shall see, we shall see. But, upon my word, Monsieur, you are far too indulgent towards her.

RICHELIEU. Sire, leave severity to your ministers; forgiveness is a royal virtue.

KING. Yes . . . I know, I know. Well, so be it. I leave you to set the date and make all the arrangements?

RICHELIEU. Yes, Sire. You should, however, bring the Queen the news yourself. It will make her so very happy.

KING. You think so?

RICHELIEU. With certainty, your Majesty.

KING. Very well. I'll go to her now.

RICHELIEU. It's the right thing to do.

KING. Yes, I know.

RICHELIEU. By the way, Sire, do not forget to tell Her Majesty that, at the ball, you wish her to wear her diamonds. She will greatly appreciate your interest. Women need these little assurances now and then.

KING. Yes, yes, very well. *(Exiting.)* You know King's can use little assurances now and then as well.

RICHELIEU. Of course, your Majesty. *(King exits. Jussac enters.)*

JUSSAC. From London, your Grace. *(Hands him a letter.)* From Milady de Winter.

RICHELIEU *(Reading)*. "I have acquired the two items you requested but am unable to leave London for want of money. Send me five hundred pistoles and four or five days after I have received them I will be in Paris." Excellent. Jussac.

JUSSAC. Your Grace?

RICHELIEU. Inform the King that her Majesty's ball will take place exactly two weeks from today, then meet me in my chambers. You're going to London again. *(Exit.)*

Scene 14

(A room in the Louvre. Queen Anne and Constance enter. The Queen, visibly upset.)

ANNE. No, he insisted I wear them! Urged on, no doubt, by the Cardinal. Someone is betraying me! I know it! *(She grabs Constance violently and looks in her eyes.)* Constance?

CONSTANCE. Upon my soul, Madame, I would die before betraying your confidence.

ANNE *(Beat)*. Forgive me. Forgive me, my dear Constance.

CONSTANCE. Madame, now is not the time to despair. We must get the diamonds back.

ANNE. Who could we possibly trust?

CONSTANCE. Trust me, Madame. I will find a messenger. A few words and your seal will do.

ANNE *(Writing)*. Yes. Yes.

CONSTANCE. My husband is a man who neither hates nor loves anybody. He will do anything I wish. I can

convince him to set out for London and deliver your letter
without him ever knowing what he's carrying. I assure
you, Madame, he will do as I ask.

ANNE. Do this and you will have saved my life . . .
and my honor. *(About to give her the letter.)* These few words
could mean my life.

CONSTANCE. Only if they fall into the wrong
hands. Give me the letter, Madame, the time is short.

(They exit.)

Scene 15

*(Monsieur Bonacieux's Inn.   A servant cleaning.
Bonacieux is seeing Rochefort out.)*

ROCHE. You understand, of course, that there are
political moves and then there are criminal acts -

BONACIEUX *(Handing Roche. a glass of wine).*   Of
course.

ROCHE.   Thank you, Monsieur - and the
unfortunate abduction of your wife was, of course, merely
a political move.   But I'm sure you understand these
matters. The Cardinal informs me that you have quite a
sophisticated political sense.

BONACIEUX. Well, well . . . he flatters me a trifle, I
dare say.

ROCHE. Oh, come now, it's not everyone of whom
the Cardinal speaks so highly.

BONACIEUX. I'm a simple man, Monsieur.

ROCHE. And a humble one.

BONACIEUX. Well.

70

ROCHE. I may call on you again, mayn't I?

BONACIEUX. Please, my house is always open to you.

ROCHE. If you think of anything else, or hear from your wife, please feel free to call on me.

BONACIEUX. Of course.

ROCHE *(Bowing)*. Monsieur.

BONACIEUX *(Bowing)*. Monsieur. *(Calling after.)* My best to the Cardinal! Pleasant fellow. I must to my thoughts political. The bourgeoisie shall be heard. If I am called upon to be their voice, so be it. Who am I to resist the Cardinal. *(Constance enters.)* My dear Constance! You're safe! *(Rushes to her, arms open.)*

CONSTANCE *(Presenting her cheek to him)*. We must talk.

BONACIEUX. That's all you have to say to me after being gone for so long?

CONSTANCE. What I have to tell you is of great importance.

BONACIEUX. Well, I have something of no little importance to tell you also.

CONSTANCE. Obey my instructions and you may -

BONACIEUX. Obey you?

CONSTANCE. There is a great deal of money to be gained.

BONACIEUX. Go on.

CONSTANCE. You must set out immediately to London. I will give you a letter which you must not part with on any account, and which you will deliver into the proper hands.

BONACIEUX. I have no business in London.

CONSTANCE. But another does.

BONACIEUX. Who, pray?

CONSTANCE. I cannot say.

BONACIEUX.   Then I cannot go. No more intrigues for me. I have tasted the Bastille and lost my appetite for such affairs. The Cardinal has enlightened me on that point.

CONSTANCE. The Cardinal! You have seen the Cardinal!?

BONACIEUX. He took my hand and called me his friend. Do you hear that Madame? I am a friend of Cardinal Richelieu, and as his servant, I cannot allow you to be involved in plots against the safety of the state.

CONSTANCE. And what do you know about the state!?

BONACIEUX. I know enough to merit this. *(Taking out his bag of money from his coat pocket.)* From the Cardinal.

CONSTANCE. You fool! You sell yourself to the devil!?

BONACIEUX. Hold your tongue, Madame! You have no political sense.

CONSTANCE. I have sense enough to know you're a coward!

(d'Artagnan sneaks in and hides himself to listen to the conversation. M. Bona. locks up his bag of money.)

BONACIEUX. Now, tell me of this affair you want me to undertake?

CONSTANCE. I can only tell you that - *(Changing her tone.)* - that I feel . . . perhaps you are right. Perhaps a man *does* know more of politics than a woman, especially one who has spoken to the Cardinal, a man such as you.

BONACIEUX. I wish only to protect you, my dear.

CONSTANCE.   Very well . . . let us say no more about it, then.

BONACIEUX.   Yes, you're quite right. *(Awkwardly.)* Pardon me, Madame, *(Starting to leave.)* but not knowing you were returning, I had made a prior engagement which requires my attention.

CONSTANCE.   As you please, sir.

BONACIEUX.   You are not angry with me?

CONSTANCE.   Not in the least, Monsieur.

BONACIEUX.   Very well. It's so wonderful to have you back. *(He goes to kiss her on the lips and she again offers her cheek. He kisses her hand instead.)* Madame *(He exits.)*

CONSTANCE *(d'Art. enters unseen to Constance).* Well, there wanted nothing more to complete that wretched creature than him becoming a Cardinalist!

D'ART *(Stepping forward).* Madame.

CONSTANCE.   Monsieur!

D'ART.   Forgive me, Madame, but I could not wait until you called on me.

CONSTANCE.   What have you overheard?

D'ART.   First, that your husband is a fool, next, that you are in trouble - which pleases me to no end because it gives me an opportunity to serve you - and lastly, that the Queen wants a brave, devoted, intelligent man to go to London for her. I possess at least two of those qualities - so here I am. Your secret will be safe with me.

CONSTANCE.   The secret is not mine to reveal.

D'ART.   You were just about to confide it to your husband.

CONSTANCE.   Yes, as one confides a letter to the collar of a dog.

D'ART. Put me to the proof. I swear to you before God, I will die sooner than do anything to compromise you or the Queen.

CONSTANCE *(Deciding)*. I yield to you, sir. You must deliver this into the hands of no one but the Duke of Buckingham and return with the item in question before the night of the Queen's ball. Have you money enough?

D'ART. None.

CONSTANCE. A moment. *(Runs to where M. Bona put his bag of money.)* Take this.

D'ART *(Enjoying this greatly)*. I shall take great pleasure in saving the Queen on the Cardinal's own money!

CONSTANCE. Shh! I hear someone. My husband!

D'ART. Quickly! Over here.

(They hide. Bona. enters with Roche. Upon seeing Roche., d'Art. half draws his sword and steps out of hiding. Constance grabs him and pulls him back.)

BONACIEUX *(To Roche)*. She's not here. She must have returned to the Louvre.

ROCHE *(To Bona)*. And you're sure she did not suspect your intentions when you left her?

BONACIEUX. Oh, she's much too shallow-minded a woman to suspect anything. The news I brought you is valuable, then, yes? The Cardinal will pleased?

ROCHE. Undoubtedly. You should have accepted the mission, though, then you would have been in possession of the letter, and the Cardinal would surely have given you some title or other as recompense.

BONACIEUX. There's still time!

ROCHE. What do you mean?

BONACIEUX. I'll go to the Louvre and tell her I've changed my mind. She adores me and will do anything I say.

ROCHE. Do so quickly. I'll to his Grace. *(He exits.)*

BONACIEUX *(Discovering his money is gone, he let's out a howl)*. I've been robbed! Thieves! Thieves! They've taken my money! Help! *(Running out.)* Someone help me! I've been robbed! Help! *(His howling continues as he runs off.)*

CONSTANCE *(To d'Art)*. He'll rouse the whole quarter! You must go at once! I'll return to the Louvre. Courage, my friend, but, above all, keep safe. Remember you belong now to the Queen.

D'ART. To her and to you. I promise you I will return worthy of both the Queen's gratitude, and your love. *(Exits.)*

Scene 16

(A street in Paris. The Three Musketeers, letters in hand)

ATHOS. You, too, then?

ARAMIS. Yes.

ATHOS. This is very strange. When did you receive yours?

ARAMIS. This morning.

ATHOS. Porthos?

PORTHOS. I was with Aramis. Both were delivered at the same time.

ATHOS. This is very unlike Monsieur Treville.

ARAMIS. And all three of us to receive them at the same time.

PORTHOS. I don't like it. *(Enter d'Artagnan.)* Since when do Musketeers receive furloughs without them being asked for?

D'ART *(Entering with Planchet. Planchet struggling with luggage).* Since the moment they have friends to ask it for them. Stay here, Planchet. *(Planchet drops bags.)*

ATHOS. Is it you, then, who is behind all this?

D'ART. It is.

ARAMIS. And what does it all mean?

D'ART. It means we're going to London, gentlemen.

PORTHOS. London!?

PLANCHET. London?

PORTHOS. What the devil are we going to do in London?

D'ART. That is a thing, my friends, I am not at liberty to tell you.

PORTHOS. Here we go again.

ATHOS. On the King's service?

D'ART. Or the Queen's.

PORTHOS. But we need money to go to London. I haven't any.

ARAMIS. Nor I.

ATHOS. Nor I.

D'ART *(Taking out Bona.'s bag of gold).* Well, I have. Three hundred pistoles worth. *(Tossing the bag to Planchet.)* Planchet, hold this.

ARAMIS. Where on earth did you get it?

D'ART. Sorry, gentlemen, I am not at liberty. It should be more than enough to get us there and back.

PORTHOS *(To Planchet of the money bag).* Stop breathing on it like that!

D'ART. Besides, I wouldn't worry - in all probability some of us will never reach London.

PORTHOS. Pardon me?

D'ART. I believe the Cardinal would give anything in the world to stop this enterprise.

PORTHOS. Well, now that I know we're at risk being killed it's much more appealing to me. But since we may be killed, I should like to know at least - if you are at liberty - *what for?*

ARAMIS. I must confess I am somewhat of Porthos' opinion.

D'ART. Does the King usually give you a reason to be killed? No. He says to you, very simply, 'Gentlemen, there is fighting in Flanders, go and fight.' And you go.

ATHOS. d'Artagnan is right. Let us go and be killed wherever we're told. Life is too short to ask so many questions. d'Artagnan, I am ready to follow you.

ARAMIS. And I.

PORTHOS. Oh, very well. I could use some exercise.

ATHOS. When do we leave?

D'ART. Immediately.

ATHOS. The plan?

D'ART. First to Calais, then the shortest route to London. I am the bearer of a letter. I cannot make copies of it because it is sealed. The letter is here - in this pocket. It must reach its destination: the Duke of Buckingham. If I should be killed, one of you will take it, and continue on; if he is killed, it will be another's turn, and so on. Agreed?

ATHOS AND ARAMIS AND PORTHOS. Agreed.

PORTHOS. I should, however, like to volunteer to be the *last* in your succession of letter carriers.

D'ART. Planchet! *(To the others.)* We have sworn, gentlemen, once and forever, explicit devotedness to each other - *all for one,* yes? Then . . . let us put it to the proof.

(They all exit.)

Scene 17

(The Cardinal, papers in hand, Rochefort and the Count de Wardes enter.)

RICHELIEU. I want every port sealed! No one is to cross the channel without my written permission. I want men on every road, every Inn, and every port. I want them stopped, gentlemen. Do we understand each other?

WARDES. Yes, your Grace.

ROCHE. Yes, your Grace.

RICHELIEU. Why wasn't I told of these furloughs!? Am I surrounded by imbeciles?! Three of the King's Musketeers and this d'Artagnan fellow granted leaves at the same time and nobody thought that suspicious!?

GUARD 1 *(Entering)*. Your Eminence.

RICHELIEU. What!?

GUARD 1. A Monsieur Jacques-Michel Bonacieux to see you.

RICHELIEU. Put him in the Bastille. He is of no use to me anymore.

GUARD 1. And afterward, Your Grace?

RICHELIEU. Once in the Bastille, there is no afterward. Do as I have ordered! De Wardes, you will to Calais, from there to London and find Milady, the Countess de Winter. I believe you know her rather well - quite intimately if I'm not mistaken. She is to return immediately. Rochefort.

ROCHE. Your Grace.

RICHELIEU.   See to it that they never reach
London.

(INTERMISSION.)

ACT II

Scene 18

(A port at Calais. A busy dock. Men carrying luggage and supplies across the stage. A few passengers wait in a line to board a ship; the Captain looking at their papers at the head of the line. Rochefort enters with four or five Guardsmen.)

ROCHE *(Positioning his Guards).* Two of you wait here. You, take the other end. *(To the captain, handing him a paper.)* Sir, this edict is to be strictly enforced starting immediately. From direct order of the Cardinal.

CAPTAIN *(Reading).* But, Monsieur, my passengers are booked already; we sail within the hour.

ROCHE. You have passengers on board already?

CAPTAIN. Yes, sir.

ROCHE *(To two other Guards).* You two, with me. *(They exit on to the ship.)*

PASSENGER *(To Captain).* Is there a problem, Monsieur?

CAPTAIN. These orders just arrived. No one is to cross the channel without express permission from the Cardinal. *(Athos, Aramis, Porthos, Planchet and d'Art. enter.)*

PASSENGER 1. But, Monsieur, I have urgent business in England!

CAPTAIN. Gentlemen, Gentlemen, you heard the orders.

PORTHOS *(To Aramis and d'Art).* What's all this?

ARAMIS. Our friends again. The Cardinal's Guards.

ATHOS. Cloaks, gentlemen. *(They conceal their swords with their cloaks.)*

D'ART *(Of the Guards)*. I count three of them.

ATHOS. Aramis, see what's going on.

(Aramis joins the group by the Captain. At this same moment, Rochefort and his Guards come back on stage, bringing with him a few passengers that they are expelling from the ship.)

PASSENGER *(To Rochefort)*. This is ridiculous, Monsieur!

ROCHE. Complain to the Cardinal.

CAPTAIN *(To Roche)*. Sir, I appeal to you, all of these gentlemen have been approved for travel by the Governor of the Port, their money is paid, their luggage already stowed.

ROCHE. Un-stow it. *(To the Captain.)* Sir, I leave you to your duty. *(To two of his Guards.)* You two with me. *(They exit.)*

D'ART *(Having seen it's Rochefort who is talking)*. There he is again! YOU!!

PORTHOS. Shh!

D'ART. It's him! It's that damned - ! *(Athos puts a hand over his mouth and restrains him.)*

ATHOS. Quiet! This is not the time! Remember why you're here.

CAPTAIN. Gentlemen. Those of you without a writ of passage; there is another ship just now arrived from England. She sails again in two days.

ARAMIS *(Returning)*. No one leaves France without written permission from the Cardinal.

PORTHOS. Now what do we do?

WARDES (*Who has entered behind the Musketeers*).
Excuse me, gentlemen.

ALL. Sir. Monsieur. *Etc.*

WARDES. What seems to be the problem?

PORTHOS. No one crosses the channel without permission from the Cardinal.

WARDES. Oh. Thank you, sir. *(Holding up a paper.)* I have that permission. Good day.

D'ART *(All four of the men look at each other. Then, to Wardes)*. Excuse me, sir.

WARDES. Yes?

D'ART. I wonder if I might ask a favor of you?

WARDES. Sir?

D'ART. Well, I'd rather like to have that letter of permission of yours.

WARDES. You are joking, I assume.

D'ART. You assume incorrectly.

WARDES. Let me pass, sir.

D'ART. I'm afraid I can't allow that.

WARDES. Since you will have it so. *(They fight.)*

ARAMIS *(Watching d'Art)*. He has quite an unorthodox style of fighting, hasn't he?

ATHOS. Quite.

PORTHOS. Seems to work, though, doesn't it?

PLANCHET *(To Athos and Aramis of the Cardinal's Guards)*. Gentlemen. Behind you.

ATHOS AND ARAMIS AND PORTHOS. Oh. *(Engaging the three Guards.)*

ARAMIS. Thank you, Planchet.

(d'Art. makes rather quick work of Wardes, but is slightly wounded as he does. As de Wardes falls, d'Art. takes the letter of permission from his pocket. Aramis

*and Athos drop their cloaks and engage the Guards.
Aramis dispatches one Guard. Porthos fights the other.
Athos toys with his opponent until d'Art. safely has the
letter of permission.)*

ATHOS *(Still fighting, but talking to d'Art).* d'Artagnan!
When I dispatch this fellow, engage with me!

D'ART. What?

ATHOS *(Dispatches the Guard and begins fighting with
d'Artagnan).* Come now, make a good show of it!

D'ART *(Catching on).* You scoundrel! I serve the
Cardinal! *(They have a brief exchange and Athos rushes out as if
in flight.)* Coward!

CAPTAIN. My good sir, are you hurt?

D'ART. Not terribly, no. That villain tried to steal
my travel orders.

CAPTAIN. You have permission to sail then, sir?

D'ART. I am a faithful servant of the Cardinal,
Monsieur. *(Handing him DeWardes' paper.)*

CAPTAIN *(Reading).* Your name, sir? *(d'Art. has not
read the letter yet, so he doesn't know what name to give. Planchet
looks over the shoulder of the Captain and reads it.)*

D'ART. My name, sir. I . . .

PLANCHET. Excuse me, Captain, but may I put the
Count de Wardes' luggage on board?

CAPTAIN. My apologies, Monsieur de Wardes.
Welcome aboard, we sail presently.

D'ART. Thank you, Monsieur. *(Privately.)* Thank
you, Planchet.

*(As d'Art. exits passengers just arrived from another
ship cross the stage. Among them is Milady and Kitty
having just returned from England, being escorted by*

*Rochefort. Milady catches d'Art.'s eye just as he is about
to exit on to the ship. Kitty sees d'Art. also. The
Captain ushers d'Art. on to the ship.)*

ROCHE. This way, Milady. His Grace didn't expect
you back so soon. Have you the - ?
MILADY *(As De Winter enters)*. Quiet.
ROCHE. My Lord de Winter. What an unexpected
pleasure. What brings you to France?
WINTER. Curiosity. What brings you to Calais?
ROCHE. Business. With your lordship's sister.
WINTER. I pray, do not mock me, sir, I think you
mean with my brother's widow.
ROCHE. Indeed, Monsieur, we are truly sorry for
your loss.
WINTER. Yes. *(Exiting ahead of Milady and Rochefort.)*
Madame?
MILADY. A moment, my lord. *(Gesturing for Kitty to
follow after Winter.)* Kitty.
ROCHE. What is he doing here?
MILADY. He fancies himself my guardian now that
his brother's dead - rest easy; he knows nothing.
ROCHE. Did you get what you wanted in London?
MILADY. Monsieur, I always get what I want.

(They exit.)

Scene 19

*(London. The Duke of Buckingham's Palace.
Buckingham is speaking to a nobleman.)*

BUCK. I will present your concerns to the King this afternoon in open council. England's hand shall not be forced in this affair.

NOBLE. What answer then shall I return to the Protestants a La Rochelle? *(Patrick enters.)*

BUCK. A moment, please.

PATRICK. Your Grace, a young man from France has arrived. He swears he will not leave your door until you see him.

BUCK. Who is he?

PATRICK. He will say only that he is the young man who sought a quarrel with you one night in Paris.

BUCK. Good heavens! Send him in at once. *(To the Nobleman.)* You must excuse me, my lord. A matter of some urgency has just developed.

NOBLE. Certainly, Your Grace. *(Exits.)*

BUCK *(To Nobleman)*. My apologies. *(d'Art. enters with Patrick.)*

D'ART. Your Grace, I -

BUCK *(Buck. takes d'Art. aside)*. Has anything happened to the Queen? Is she safe?

D'ART. Yes, but I believe her to be in grave danger.

BUCK. What is it? Speak, man!

D'ART. Pray, take this letter, Your Grace.

BUCK *(Reading)*. Is it even so . . . *(He takes off the diamonds that he is wearing under his outer garment.)* . . . here. Here is the precious gift that I vowed should be buried with me. The Queen gave them me, the Queen takes them back. Return these immediately to her - *(Noticing that two of them are missing.)* God in heaven!

D'ART. What is it, your Grace!?

BUCK. Two of them are missing! The diamonds! There are but ten! *(Ruminating.)* When does the Queen need the diamonds?

D'ART. By Monday next.

BUCK. Five days. More than enough time. Patrick! Fetch my jeweler and the secretary. *(Buckingham writes.)* Someone stole those diamonds; if they have not yet left England, they never will.

D'ART. How so, Your Grace?

BUCK. This is an embargo. No ship will sail without my express permission. *(The jeweler enters.)* Mr. Reilly, how long and how much will it take you to make two diamonds to match these others?

REILLY. Well . . . *(looking at diamonds.)* . . . worth about three thousand a piece . . . at least a week, my lord.

BUCK. You will have six thousand a piece and I will have them in my hands the day after tomorrow.

REILLY. Yes, Your Grace. *(The secretary enters. Jeweler exits.)*

BUCK. Mr. Jackson, go instantly to the Lord Chancellor and have him execute these orders. Say I am determined on war, and that this measure is my first act of hostility against France.

JACKSON. Yes, Your Grace. *(Jackson exits.)*

BUCK *(To d'Art).* And now, my friend, is there anything I can do for you?

D'ART. Let us understand each other, my lord. What I have done has been for my Queen, and France, and not at all for your Grace. At this moment, if there is a question of war, I see nothing in you but an Englishman, and consequently, an enemy.

BUCK. Perhaps another time, then. *(Ushering him off.)* Sir.

(They exit.)

Scene 20

(France. The night of the royal ball. The stage is peopled with nobles and ladies of high society. The ball has been going on for some time. Soldiers standing guard, musicians playing, people laughing and mingling. Masks are handed out to people if they don't have them. Loud cries and cheers are heard as the King enters with associates, and Treville.)

KING *(Preoccupied)*. I apologize, everyone, for my late arrival. Monsieur the Cardinal once again has kept me detained with affairs of state.

CHESNAYE. This way, Your Majesty. *(Leading the King to choose his mask.)*

KING. Inform me the moment the Cardinal arrives.

JUSSAC. Yes, my Lord.

(The Queen enters with Constance. Cheers and a commotion are heard again as people rush to meet her. She receives them politely. She is not wearing her diamonds. At the same moment, the Cardinal enters above, dressed as a Spanish cavalier. He watches the Queen. Behind him we see Milady and Rochefort, when they enter below they will be masked. Lord De Winter is also present.)

KING *(Seeing the Queen, he throws down his mask)*. Get this ridiculous thing off me! *(He makes his way through the crowd to confront the Queen. The Cardinal has entered below and intercepts him.)* How now, Monsieur!

RICHELIEU *(Handing the King a small box).* Your Majesty.

KING. What do you mean by this?

RICHELIEU. Oh, nothing, my lord, only if the Queen is wearing her diamonds, which I very much doubt, count them and if you find only ten, ask Her Majesty who could have stolen the two that I have here.

(The King goes to confront the Queen, but before he has a chance, a dance begins. The King, the Queen, Rochefort, Milady and all others all dance. It is a stately dance which exchanges partners. The King tries to get a look at the Queen to see if she's wearing the diamonds, but she keeps getting passed along before he can. As the dance progresses, it is obvious that the Queen will shortly be passed into the hands of the King. A phrase or two before that is to happen, d'Artagnan, masked, rushes into the ball, frantically searching for the Queen. He spots her, pulls out a nobleman from the dance and becomes the next partner whom the Queen is passed to. As he dances with the Queen, he places the diamonds around her neck. Constance seeing this, helps. Milady sees all this. The King is the Queen's next partner. As they meet each other, the King sees she is wearing the diamonds.)

ANNE. Your Majesty. *(The King stops dancing. The music stops abruptly. The crowd can tell something is amiss and they respectfully keep their distance.)*

KING. Madame, I believe two of your diamonds are missing, and I am here giving them back to you. *(Holds out the box the Cardinal gave him.)*

ANNE. My Lord, are you giving me yet another two? But then I shall have fourteen! *(The King counts the diamonds.)* It's really too much, your Majesty.

KING. Richelieu!

RICHELIEU. Sire. *(Richelieu glares at Milady as he approaches.)*

KING. Be kind enough to inform me what this means?

RICHELIEU. It means . . . Sire . . . that I wished to present the Queen with this gift, and not daring to present it myself, I adopted these means of inducing her to accept them. Madame, I would be most grateful if you would do me the honor of accepting them.

ANNE *(To Richelieu, with a knowing smile)*. I am the more grateful Monsieur, for I am certain these two diamonds cost you much more dearly than all the other twelve.

KING *(To Richelieu)*. I will speak with you in my chambers. Presently.

(The crowd bows as the King exits, aware that the ball is now over. Music stops. People take off their masks, mingle a bit in confusion, and eventually make their way off during the following scenes.)

RICHELIEU *(To Milady as he passes by. Quietly livid)*. You have deceived me, Madame.

MILADY. Indeed, Your Grace, I have not. Those diamonds I cut myself from the doublet of Buckingham.

(Gesturing to d'Artagnan.) That man there is somehow to blame.

RICHELIEU *(To Milady).* Find out who he is.

(Constance pulls d'Artagnan downstage. She has been wearing a black velvet mask.)

D'ART *(Constance takes off her mask).* Constance! At last!

CONSTANCE. Shh! *(She has pulled him down to meet the Queen. d'Artagnan falls to his knees before her.)* Your Majesty, Monsieur d'Artagnan.

ANNE. Sir . . . your devotion has not gone unnoticed. Constance. *(The Queen exits, Constance and others trailing behind her.)*

D'ART *(Stopping her, discreetly).* When shall I see you again?!

CONSTANCE. Within the hour. Outside the servants entrance. I have many thanks to offer you, but, for now, I must go.

D'ART. Yes. Yes! *(She exits. Milady and Rochefort follow her out.)*

TREVILLE. D'Artagnan.

D'ART. Sir.

TREVILLE. Monsieur Athos stays at my house. Will you come with me?

D'ART. I have an engagement first.

TREVILLE. Ah . . . the young lady? I will tell your friends, then, to expect you later. *(He exits.)*

D'ART. Thank you, Monsieur. *(He exits.)*

Scene 21

(Outside the Louvre where d'Artagnan is to meet Constance. Rochefort and another man or two are dragging Constance across the stage. She is bound, gagged and wrapped in a cloak.)

MILADY *(Following close behind).* See that she doesn't escape this time, or the Cardinal will have both our heads. Or must I do everything myself?

ROCHE. I will tend to her personally, Milady.

MILADY. Not too personally. Find out what you can and come to me tonight. *(She sees Winter about to enter.)* Go now. *(To Winter)* My lord! Where have you been? I've been searching all over for you.

WINTER. And I for you, Madame.

MILADY *(Putting on the mask she has taken from Constance).* Well . . . we seem to have found each other . . . haven't we? *(Seeing d'Artagnan, she grabs Winter.)* Why do you keep following me, sir?! I beg you to leave me in peace. I have done nothing to deserve this! *(d'Artagnan rushes on to help, thinking Milady is Constance.)*

WINTER *(Attempting to push her away).* Are you mad?

MILADY. Take your hands from me, sir!

D'ART. Constance! Behind me! *(Sword drawn, he backs Winter away from Milady.)* Your name and business, sir, or your sword. *(Winter draws. They fight.)*

MILADY. *(Feigning fright.)* Gentlemen!

(After a brief exchange, d'Artagnan disarms Winter. Winter steps back and falls. d'Art. stands over Winter, sword at his throat.)

91

D'ART. I could kill you, Monsieur. Cry mercy of
Madame Bonacieux and I will, perhaps, spare your life.
WINTER. Sir, you are mistaken.
D'ART. And you, sir, are a corpse if you do not -
MILADY. Monsieur, you *are* mistaken.
D'ART. Milady! *(He keeps the sword at Winter's throat.)*
MILADY. You know me then?
D'ART. I have seen you, Madame. And heard of
you.
MILADY. And I of you. Yes. That man you are
about to kill is my brother-in-law, Lord de Winter, Baron
of Sheffield. We were having a little family quarrel.
WINTER *(To d'Art).* Sir.
D'ART. Monsieur. *(Noticing his sword at Winter's
throat, takes it away and helps him up.)* Oh, I - my apologies,
sir. I thought . . . I saw you and the lady struggling and I
. . .

WINTER. No apologies, Monsieur. I am indebted
to you for sparing my life.
MILADY. As am I, sir.
D'ART. I was to meet a lady friend at this very spot,
and I thought, upon seeing you, that -
MILADY. Oh, heavens! A lady!?
D'ART. Yes.
MILADY. About my size, dark hair, lovely features?
D'ART. Yes.
MILADY. Oh God, it was she! Wasn't it Lord de
Winter!?
WINTER. Who?
MILADY. We were just leaving the ball when we
heard screams.
D'ART. Screams?

MILADY. Yes. A woman's. We hurried here to see what the matter was, and . . .

D'ART. Yes?!

MILADY. When we arrived we saw a young woman, as I described to you, bound, gagged and being forced into a carriage by three men.

D'ART. Did you see any of the men, their faces? Do you know any of them?

MILADY. Only one, sir, have I seen before. I don't know his name - a distinguished looking gentleman but for a scar across his face -

D'ART. AH!! Forever he! Damn him!

MILADY. Your lady friend did not appear harmed in any way. That is well.

D'ART. Indeed. Excuse me, Madame, but I must see what I can do to help. It has been a pleasure meeting you. (To Winter.) My lord. (d'Art. starts to exit.)

MILADY. Pray, pardon me, Monsieur, but perhaps I can be of some help. I am not at all in bad favor at the court; a word here and there might be of some service to you. We can discuss the matter at more length at my home. No. 6 Rue Royale. Eight o'clock. Tomorrow night. Shall I expect you, Monsieur . . . ?

D'ART. D'Artagnan. I would be honored, Madame.

MILADY. Very good. Till then.

D'ART. Milady. Sir. (He exits.)

MILADY. Brother.

(A beat from Winter. He walks away from Milady.)

Scene 22

(Late. Treville's Palace. Enter Treville and Athos. Athos a bit drunk.)

ATHOS. He is well, then? Our young champion?

TREVILLE. Quite well.

ATHOS. Yes. He's happy. He's in Paris. He's twenty.

TREVILLE. He's also in danger. It seems our young friend has thwarted some design or other of the Cardinal's. It will, as you know, not go unanswered - are you ill, my friend?

ATHOS. No, no, just an old wound. It bothers me now and then.

TREVILLE. Well, have my surgeon look at it. *(Exiting.)* Rest well; the English are reinforcing the Protestants at La Rochelle. We join the siege within the month.

ATHOS. Yes, Captain.

TREVILLE. And see to that wound. *(Exits.)*

ATHOS. Yes, Captain, *(Pouring a glass of wine.)* I will. *(He drinks.)*

(d'Artagnan enters as Treville exits. They meet at the entranceway.)

TREVILLE. Monsieur. I didn't expect you here so early.

D'ART. My rendezvous took a rather unexpected turn.

TREVILLE. They often do. I leave you to your friend. Monsieur. *(Exits.)*

D'ART. My dear Athos! *(Embracing Athos.)* I'm so happy to see you well! My mission to England was a complete success. Thanks to you. Tell me, how fared we at Calais?

ATHOS. Well enough; all are mostly sound. Porthos was wounded - posteriorly. He maintains, however, that he turned his ankle.

D'ART. And Aramis?

ATHOS. Oh, Aramis . . . he with the weight of the world and the salvation of all humankind on his shoulders . . . he was slightly wounded, and while recuperating remembered that he was a Musketeer only *temporarily* and decided to take Holy Orders again.

D'ART. Is he serious this time?

ATHOS. He's serious every time. He fasted for three days, claiming his wound was a warning from heaven for him to return to his Mother Church. His wound, though, as always with him, was one inflicted by a woman not a sword. He'd been pining over his latest mistress who hadn't answered his letters. Fortunately, I had with me a letter from this very lady. Upon reading it, he sprang out of bed, called for wine, renounced the church, began writing poetry, and I haven't seen him since. These women give us more trouble than Spain and England combined.

D'ART *(Beat)*. You're talkative.

ATHOS. I'm drunk, of which talking is an unfortunate side effect.

D'ART. Well, I shall take advantage of the fact. I worry about you, Athos.

ATHOS. And I of you; but fear not, drunkards and lovers fall under care of the same protective deity.

D'ART. Let us hope so, for my dear Constance has been abducted again.

ATHOS. It's becoming a habit with the woman.

D'ART. I met a woman who witnessed it and thinks she can be of some help.

ATHOS. Another woman is involved? Who is she?

D'ART. Milady de Winter. The same woman I saw at the inn when I first came to Paris.

ATHOS. You've just lost one woman and now you're after another!?

D'ART. No. I'm only trying to divine what part she plays in all this. I'm sure she didn't even recognize me.

ATHOS. There is no such thing as *surety* where women are concerned.

D'ART. When I have learned what I need to know, I will leave her.

ATHOS. Leaving a woman is easier said than done, my friend. Don't be a fool.

D'ART. You know, you might be a little more supportive.

ATHOS. You might be a little more wise. Come, tell me more of this woman.

(They exit.)

Scene 23

(Milady's chambers. Milady and Rochefort)

ROCHE. De Winter leaves Paris tonight

MILADY. Thank God. How on earth did you contrive it?

ROCHE. Oh, an unforeseen claim on his family estate suddenly appeared in the courts of England.

MILADY. You can be so delightfully wicked when you put your mind to it.

ROCHE. You flatter me, Madame. But of course, *you* devised his poor brother's death, I merely claimed his lands.

MILADY. *My* lands, you mean - once de Winter is taken off for good.

ROCHE. In good time, Madame, in good time. Now, shall I remain to give you some help with this troublesome Gascon?

MILADY. You underestimate me, Monsieur; the fool was mine at first glance.

ROCHE. I believe him to be no fool, Madame.

MILADY. What? Are you jealous, my friend?

KITTY *(Entering)*. Excuse me, Madame. Monsieur d'Artagnan has arrived.

MILADY. Show him in.

MILADY *(To Roche)*. You will excuse me, Monsieur.

ROCHE. Invariably. *(He exits.)*

KITTY *(Entering with d'Art. behind)*. This way, sir. Madame. Monsieur d'Artagnan.

MILADY. Monsieur, welcome to my home.

D'ART. Madame.

MILADY. I'm so glad you're here. How are you? Any news of your dear friend, Madame..?

D'ART. Bonacieux. Constance Bonacieux.

MILADY. Yes. Yes. Any developments?

D'ART. No, Madame.

MILADY. Pity. I will take the matter up with my friends at court. I'm sure they can help.

D'ART. I thank you, Madame.

MILADY. No need to thank me. I know what it is to lose a loved one.

D'ART. Yes?

MILADY. My husband - my late husband, Lord de Winter's brother - died very unexpectedly not long after we were married, leaving me in a strange country with very little hope and even less future. Lord de Winter has been kind enough to look after me these past few months. *(Moved.)* I'm sorry. And you?

D'ART. Madame?

MILADY. Where are you from? What brought you to Paris?

D'ART. I am from Bearn, Madame, in Gascony. I came to Paris to join the King's Musketeers.

MILADY. I see. Have you ever been to England?

D'ART. No, Madame, I have not had the pleasure. Madame?

MILADY. I'm sorry. You remind me of someone I once knew. *(Beat.)* Shall we go in? I should like to hear more about you - and your friend, Madame Bonacieux.

D'ART. Of course, Milady.

MILADY. I do love when you call me that. Pray, do so from now on. *(Calling off.)* Kitty! Monsieur, please see yourself to drawing room. I will attend you presently.

D'ART. Milady. *(Kisses her hand. Exits.)*

KITTY. Madame?

MILADY. See that no one disturbs us tonight. Help me here. *(Kitty helps: hair or gown.)*

KITTY. Yes, Madame. He's quite handsome. *(D'Artagnan returns for his hat. Stops, and overhears Milady.)* Does your ladyship love him?

MILADY. Love him? I detest the imbecile. The coward held Lord de Winter's life in his hands and didn't kill him, and so lost me an inheritance of three hundred thousand a year! And I will have my revenge on him for making me lose credit with the Cardinal. He very nearly cost me my head.

KITTY. I see, Madame.

MILADY. He'll regret the day he ever crossed my path.

KITTY. Yes, Madame.

MILADY. But for now . . . I must let him play the lover.

KITTY. But I thought he . . . does he not have a mistress? The woman you took away?

MILADY. What, his dear Constance? He's already forgotten she ever existed. *(D'Art exits.)* There's a lover's revenge for you! She's not gone a day and he's kissing my hand and quivering in my drawing room. I should join him before he breaks something.

(Milady exits in the direction of the drawing room. Kitty Exits.)

Scene 24

(A street in Paris. Athos, Aramis, Porthos, and Planchet.)

PLANCHET. No, Monsieur, he told me only to gather you here at exactly four o'clock or I would receive lively thrashing.

PORTHOS. Must **we** always meet under such mystery? It's getting quite tiresome.

ARAMIS.   I've not seen d'Artagnan in a week. Athos?

ATHOS.   I've spoken to him, but in spite of my counsels - and I believe his own conscience - he continues to visit this woman, Milady de Winter.

PLANCHET.   He hasn't missed a day in two weeks. He has me cleaning his doublet on a daily basis.

ARAMIS.   He's in love with her.

PLANCHET.   He swears no.

PORTHOS.   He lies.

ARAMIS.   What do we know of her?

ATHOS.   Only this; she is certainly in league with the Cardinal. d'Artagnan's determined to play out the game.

PORTHOS.   Well, he needs to play a little quicker, for Dessarts' company marches in the morning.

ATHOS.   Yes - as do we. *(Handing them papers.)* Gentlemen, your orders. We leave at dawn.

PORTHOS.   I'm ready.

ARAMIS.   As am I.

ATHOS *(Of Aramis' books, study materials)*.   Aramis, you're not carrying all that, are you?

ARAMIS.   No, Planchet is. *(Giving him a bag or two.)* I'm translating St. Augustine. I hope the siege will last long enough for me to complete it.

PORTHOS.   Good God, I hope not.

PLANCHET *(To Aramis)*.   Sir, I happen to be in the employ of -

PORTHOS *(To Planchet)*.   Did I say you could speak? *(Seeing d'Art.)* Here's the mystery man now.

D'ART.   Gentlemen, thank you for obliging me.

PORTHOS *(To Aramis)*.   Cupid have mercy, the boy is still alive.

D'ART. And very much so, my friend - Planchet, return home, quickly, and pack my bags.

PLANCHET. I believe I have bags enough, Master. They -

PORTHOS *(To Planchet)*. Get along, you putrefied pack-horse!

PLANCHET. But, Monsieur, I am not obliged to -

PORTHOS *(Threatening Planchet)*. Do you question me!? *(Planchet exits. To d'Art.)* You really need to beat that fellow more often.

D'ART. Yes. Now, to the business at hand, gentlemen. As you know, I have been entertaining Milady de Winter for some weeks now but, as of yet, have no further news on the whereabouts of Madame Bonacieux. Monsieur Treville has asked the Queen, but she knows nothing and has initiated a search herself. I have however, had a marvelous stroke of good luck.

ATHOS. How's that?

D'ART. Milady's handmaid, Kitty, I'm afraid, has become quite enamored of me.

PORTHOS. Well, that's three now . . . how many women can you juggle, dear boy?

D'ART. I am taking advantage of her affection only to encourage her to spy on Milady de Winter.

PORTHOS. Who is it that you actually *do* love?

D'ART. Porthos, please. Kitty meets me here with a letter she says is sure to be of great import to me.

ARAMIS. Pardon me, my friend, but why share your intrigues with us now?

ATHOS. Yes, we leave for La Rochelle at dawn. As do you.

D'ART. If the letter has news of Constance, I will make a move on Milady this night, and may very well be in need of your help.

PORTHOS *(Seeing Kitty enter. To d'Art).* I believe your soubrette has arrived.

KITTY *(To d'Art).* Monsieur. *(To the rest.)* Gentlemen.

ALL *(Bowing).* Madame.

KITTY *(To D'art. Motioning him to step away from his friends).* Sir, I have a - if I may . . . sir?

D'ART. Oh, yes, my sweet. Gentlemen, excuse me. *(He moves aside with Kitty.)*

KITTY. Monsieur, my mistress does not love you at all!

D'ART. What? Is this the news you bring me?

KITTY. It's true, sir. She loves another and hates you! I would have told you sooner, but I wanted proof, and now I have it. *(Handing him a letter.)* Forgive this indiscretion of mine, sir, but in love . . . each for herself.

D'ART. *(Reading aloud.)* Monsieur le Count de Wardes.

KITTY. Yes, Monsieur, the Count de Wardes. Do you know him?

D'ART. I have met him once - *(Reading.)* - *"Since you left for England you have not visited me, or my chambers. My love, what keeps you from my side? If you repent your absence, the woman who gives you this note will conduct you the way to your pardon."*

KITTY. I'm sorry to be the one to tell you, sir.

D'ART. Indeed, Kitty, you are right . . . I have been a fool. *(Short pause.)* A moment, my dear. *(He rushes to the Musketeers.)* Porthos, keep the lady company. *(Porthos does. To Aramis, who has been copying his Latin.)* Aramis, your pen and paper, please!

ATHOS. What are you up to now?

D'ART *(Handing him the letter)*. Read this. *(Aramis and Athos read the letter.)* If I can't discover where Constance is . . . perhaps Milady's lover can. *(He writes.)*

ARAMIS *(Of the letter)*. How's this?

ATHOS *(Reading the letter)*. The Count de Wardes? The gentleman you very nearly killed at Calais. The one whose letter of transport you borrowed.

D'ART. Yes . . . it seems his wounds have been keeping him from his love bed.

ATHOS. What are you writing?

D'ART. Monsieur de Warde's reply . . . *(Reading.)* *"Madame: I do repent my absence and willingly submit to whatever penance you require of me at eleven o'clock tonight. I am in great danger, hence my absence. Please have your chambers darkened. I will come to you cloaked and anxious for contrition."* An indelicacy, perhaps, gentlemen, but in love . . . each for himself. *(He goes to Kitty.)*

ARAMIS. I'll pray for him

ATHOS. Do.

D'ART. Kitty, I will see Milady one more time tonight - only to tell her I shall never see her again.

KITTY. Oh, sir . . . you will be the better off.

D'ART. I hope, though, I shall again see you.

KITTY. Oh, yes, yes, sir. Yes. sir.

D'ART *(Warmly. Taking her hands)*. Will you do one more thing for me? A thing that will surely end all between Milady and me.

KITTY. Anything, sir. Yes.

D'ART. Deliver to her this letter *(Gives her the letter.)* Go now. *(He kisses her.)* Don't tell her who it is from and don't read it. Can I trust you?

KITTY. Oh, yes, sir. *(She exits.)*

D'ART *(Exiting with his friends).* Gentlemen, if you would be so kind as to meet me an hour before dawn outside No. 6 Rue Royale, I shall, perhaps, march on early with you to La Rochelle. A little lie, my friends, is sometimes required to achieve a great good.

(They exit.)

Scene 25

(That night. Milady's chambers. Milady in her night dress.)

MILADY *(Enters reading the phony letter from de Wardes letter.)* "... I will come to you cloaked and anxious for contrition." Monsieur le Cardinal forbids me to harm our little Gascon ... then my dear de Wardes shall rid me of his presence. *(A knock at the door. She opens it.)* Monsieur de Wardes? Is that you?

D'ART *(Pretending to be de Wardes).* Yes. Are you alone?

MILADY. Of course. *(d'Artagnan enters in a heavy, hooded cloak. His face is completely hidden.)* My precious boy. I've missed you. *(She attempts to kiss him. D'Art. hides his face.)* What? Suddenly shy? You're not going English on me, are you? Oh, come now, you're safe with me. You know I'm discreet, yes? *(She guides him toward the bedroom.)* Come ... I promise no one will see you, not even I. We shall have nothing between us but darkness.

(They go into the bedroom.)

Scene 26

(The Louvre. Enter Treville and the Queen.)

TREVILLE.   Forgive me, Your Majesty, for calling on you at this late hour, but I have news which will please you.

ANNE. Yes, Monsieur?

TREVILLE. We have found Madame Bonacieux.

ANNE. Oh, thank heaven. Is she well?

TREVILLE.   Yes, Madame.   Our intelligence discovered she was being held in a small garrison at the Port de La Villette.

ANNE. And where is she now?

TREVILLE. Still at La Villette. She will not be safe in Paris, Madame.

ANNE. Might we not send her abroad? .

TREVILLE. We are at war with England, Your Majesty. It's too dangerous. The Duke of Buckingham will soon set out for La Rochelle.

ANNE. Very well . . . have her escorted to the Carmelite convent at Bethune. I will give orders to the Superior to take her in as a novice under my patronage. She will be safe there.

TREVILLE. Yes, Your Majesty.

ANNE. Well done, Monsieur Treville. In the morning I will have the orders signed. See that she is treated well.

(They exit.)

Scene 27

(Milady's chambers. Just before dawn. d'Artagnan exits the bedroom, putting on his hooded cloak again. Milady follows behind him.)

MILADY *(Offering him a ring).* Monsieur, before you go, take this of me.

D'ART. Madame -

MILADY. No, no . . . keep it as a token . . . a remembrance of our night together.

D'ART. There is so much more I feel that I cannot say to you. *(Kisses her. Starts to go.)*

MILADY. My sweet. You will remember to avenge me on that arrogant Gascon, d'Artagnan, won't you?

D'ART. Trust me, Madame, I shall meet him sooner than you think.

MILADY. You will visit again soon, I hope?

D'ART. No, Madame, I shall not.

MILADY. Paris is still too dangerous?

D'ART. No, your bedchamber is still too tedious.

MILADY. What?

D'ART. I thought, perhaps, that after some absence I would have found you a trifle more appealing and our night games a little more interesting. But I was the more deceived. Madame; do not count on me for another rendezvous in the near future. When, and if, your turn comes again, I will let you know. *(He exits.)*

KITTY *(Entering).* Madame, the gentleman says you're not feeling well. Are you ill?

MILADY. How dare you touch me! Ill!! Do I look ill!?

KITTY. Madame, I -

106

MILADY. Speak again and I will cut your peasant throat! Summon Rochefort here immediately and awake the household. Now!! *(Of de Wardes.)* 'When my turn comes!?' That vile little scum, I will chop him into pieces! *(There is a banging at the door.)* Enter! *(d'Artagnan enters dressed as himself.)*

MILADY *(Overlapping)*. Monsieur d'Artagnan!

KITTY *(Overlapping)*. Monsieur d'Artagnan!

D'ART. Milady!

MILADY. What are you doing here?

D'ART. I was waiting at your gates hoping to see you this morning when I heard your screams. Are you ill?

MILADY. No I'm not ill! *(Kitty runs toward the door.)* Kitty, stop! *(Gaining her composure.)* Have breakfast prepared for Monsieur d'Artagnan and I. *(Kitty exits.)*

D'ART. Madame, I wouldn't think of intruding. No doubt you are in need of rest.

MILADY. On the contrary, stay Monsieur. I want you here . . . I need you. *(Feigning helplessness.)* You do love me, Monsieur. I am not mistaken in that, am I?

D'ART. Need you ask, Madame?

MILADY. Would you be willing to prove your love?

D'ART. Bid me do anything for you.

MILADY. I have an enemy.

D'ART. Name the villain.

MILADY. The Count de Wardes. Come to me soon and let me hear you say he does not live.

D'ART. The Count is dead. Now . . . would you be willing to prove your love for me?

MILADY. Anything. Fight de Wardes and you may have me.

D'ART *(Breaking free of her grasp)*. Madame, I have already fought de Wardes, and I have already *had* you.

MILADY. Monsieur?

D'ART.   Had you not a rendezvous with this Monsieur de Wardes just this night?

MILADY. What are you talking about?

D'ART. Rest easy, de Wardes has nothing to boast of - the ring you gave him, you see, is mine now.

MILADY. Where did you get that!?

D'ART. Why, you gave it to me, Madame, as a *"as a token . . . a remembrance of our night together."* Your own words, Milady . . . remember? You were much easier than I anticipated, Madame. I simply intercepted your letter to de Wardes - and having very nearly killed your little Count in a skirmish at Calais - I took the liberty of usurping his office. Come Madame, didn't you think the hooded cloak and darkened room was a bit much? Really. And since you were so kind as to tell me - in the throes of your passion - that Madame Bonacieux is in the garrison at the Port de La Villette, I really have no further use of you. It has been, very nearly, a pleasure, Madame.

MILADY *(As d'Art. bows, Milady violently strikes him).* You wretched scum!

(Milady attempts to strike him again. He grabs her. In this scuffle Milady's night dress is torn off her shoulders revealing a brand of the fleur-de-lis. d'Artagnan clearly sees it.)

D'ART. My God! You - the fleur-de-lis!

MILADY. You now know my secret . . . very well, then - die with it! *(She grabs a dagger.)*

(Milady rushes at d'Art. A quick, vicious struggle.)

D'ART. I'll see myself out, Madame. *(She screams and lunges for him. He exits.)*

MILADY. Guards!! Guards!! *(Guards burst into her room.)* Close the gates! Quickly! *(Running out.)* Stop standing there and do as I say you imbeciles!! *(She exits.)*

(The musketeers and Planchet enter.)

ATHOS. Do you see him anywhere?

ARAMIS. No.

ATHOS. D'Artagnan!

PORTHOS. D'Artagnan! Madman! Passion!

ATHOS. Porthos.

PORTHOS. Lover!

ATHOS. The company will march without us!

D'ART *(Entering).* Gentlemen!

PORTHOS. Where have you been?

D'ART. Looking for you!

PORTHOS. Oh.

ARAMIS *(To d'Art).* Madame Bonacieux has been found! She's safe!

D'ART. Splendid! How!?

ATHOS. The Queen! Come, we must to La Rochelle.

D'ART. Athos, I have something quite incredible to tell you.

(They exit.)

Scene 28

(The French camp at La Rochelle in front of Richelieu's quarters. Other Guards and Musketeers milling about, carrying supplies, or other preparations.)

RICHELIEU. What are the numbers?

JUSSAC. Twenty thousand. Buckingham surprised Toirac near the Ile de Re, landing nearly ninety vessels. Toirac withdrew to Saint-Martin.

RICHELIEU. And the King?

JUSSAC. Forced to halt at Villeroi with his Musketeers.

RICHELIEU. Buckingham besieges Saint-Martin and we besiege La Rochelle . . . this is no way to war.

(The three Musketeers and d'Artagnan enter. d'Artagnan and Athos in front talking privately. Treville following behind. Planchet with luggage. Other soldiers, if possible, follow behind.)

D'ART. I tell you, Athos, it was a Fleur-de-lis! Come now, are you sure that woman you spoke of is dead? How could there be more than - ? *(They notice Richelieu, stop talking, and bow.)*

RICHELIEU. Gentleman, you've arrived at last. How good of you.

TREVILLE. The King was taken ill at Villeroi, Your Grace, hence our delay. He requests your presence immediately.

RICHELIEU. Thank you, Captain. *(Seeing d'Art.)* Monsieur d'Artagnan, is it not?

D'ART. Yes, Your Grace.

RICHELIEU. I should like to speak to you. Remain here at my quarters. I will return shortly. *(He walks away with Treville.)*

D'ART. Yes, Your Grace.

ATHOS *(To d'Art)*. He knows what you look like.

ARAMIS. There's a dangerous rendezvous.

PORTHOS. I wouldn't stay.

D'ART. I have little choice, have I not?

PORTHOS. You could shoot yourself?

D'ART. I could shoot *you*.

ATHOS. Porthos, you and Aramis go on ahead. I'll stay with d'Artagnan.

PORTHOS. Planchet, take our things.

(Porthos take bags and/ or muskets of d'Art. and Athos. He deposits them on Planchet's already too-full back. They and any other soldiers exit. Athos and d'Art. continue their conversation.)

D'ART. Tell me truly, now, Athos, this lady you spoke of, the one you said was hanged, are you sure she's dead?

ATHOS. Of course she is - now stop this nonsense. It pains me to remember such things. Let us worry about your lady and what we can do for her. I think she were best to stay in the convent at Bethune until the campaign is over.

D'ART. I agree - now, listen . . . this woman - she would be about thirty, stunningly blue eyes, shapely figure -

ATHOS. And a Fleur-de-lis? Are you sure?

D'ART. Yes.

ATHOS *(Athos sees the ring d'Art. is wearing)*. Where did you get that ring?

D'ART. She gave it to me. What is it, Athos? What!?

ATHOS. My mother's ring.

D'ART. Then it is she?!

ATHOS. I must see this woman.

D'ART. Be on your guard, Athos.

ATHOS. My friend, do you, perchance, think I set any great store upon my life? It is *yours* that concerns me.

D'ART. Well, hopefully now that we are at war we shall have nothing to fear but Englishmen and muskets, and not this woman!

ATHOS. Quiet! The Cardinal. *(Athos bows and excuses himself.)* Your Grace.

(Athos appears to leave, but doubles back and conceals himself to watch over D'art. Richelieu is carrying a manuscript in his hand. He eyes d'Art. who is standing at attention.)

RICHELIEU *(Gesturing with his manuscript).* Do you ever attend the theater, my friend?

D'ART. No, Monsignor.

RICHELIEU. Pity. I flatter myself a bit of a dramatist. My newest work, *(The script.) Mirame;* a tragedy in five acts. It's not very good I'm afraid, but I am, of course, my own patron and so can afford a tragedy now and then . . . .the question is, can you?

D'ART. Your Grace?

RICHELIEU. Monsieur, I am quite aware of all of your enterprises since you came to Paris. Some of which, unfortunately, have conflicted with mine.

D'ART. Monsignor, if I have incurred your disfavor in any way, I -

RICHELIEU. Why, Monsieur, I do not punish men who carry out their orders with courage and intelligence, on the contrary, I take notice. You are brave, Monsieur, and you are also prudent, which is better. I like men of courage who can also think. You have accomplished a great deal for one so young, but you've made some powerful enemies. Therefore I believe you need guidance. What would you say to a commission in my Guards and a lieutenancy after the campaign?

D'ART *(Stunned)*. Monsignor . . . I - your kindness overwhelms me.

RICHELIEU. Very well, then.

D'ART. Your Eminence misunderstands me.

RICHELIEU. How?

D'ART. Begging your Grace's pardon, and if you will permit me to speak frankly . . .

RICHELIEU. Do.

D'ART. I am in his His Majesty's Royal Guards and hope to be transferred soon to the Musketeers. I have no reason to be dissatisfied.

RICHELIEU. Then you refuse to serve me, Monsieur? I shall not make this offer again. Very well. Remain free then, along with the hatreds that follow you.

D'ART. Monsignor, please, I -

RICHELIEU. I don't hold it against you, son. I respect your loyalties, but let me warn you: once I remove my protecting hand, your life will not be worth a sou.

D'ART. Your Grace. *(Bows and exits. Athos goes to leave his place of concealment.)*

RICHELIEU. That is unfortunate.

MILADY *(Entering)*. I think not. *(Athos stops and listens again.)*

RICHELIEU. Harp not on that string, Madame. We have more important business at hand.

MILADY. I am listening, Your Grace.

RICHELIEU. An envoy of the Duke of Buckingham has been captured. Letters taken from him confirm a league between Austria, Spain, and England. If this coalition were to triumph, Spanish and Austrian policy would quickly put an end to any influence I have over the King. I will be ruined and abandoned to the personal vengeance of Queen Anne - along with any of my followers. Do you understand my meaning?

MILADY. Yes, Your Grace.

RICHELIEU. These plans must be stopped by whatever means necessary.

MILADY. Say what you would have me do.

RICHELIEU *(Carefully)*. You will gain audience with the Duke of Buckingham.

MILADY. Your Grace remembers he suspects me of the affair with the diamonds.

RICHELIEU. Present yourself openly as my negotiator. Tell him that I know of all his allied preparations, and it disturbs me not in the least, for at the first move he makes, I shall ruin the Queen. Tell him I have proof which I will have published throughout Europe. Letters between them, sworn statements from the Queen's servants, and witnesses to his entering and leaving the Louvre.

MILADY. And what if the Duke does not relent and continues to threaten France?

RICHELIEU. Why then, I shall hope for one of those events which change the destinies of nations. Wherever there are religious differences, there will always be fanatics asking nothing more than to be made martyrs.

You know, of course, that the Puritans despise Buckingham. They call him the Antichrist. One would merely have to find a beautiful, clever woman capable of inciting some such fanatic to . . . an act of recklessness.

MILADY. I'll need an order beforehand ratifying all that I should think proper for the good of France.

RICHELIEU. Anything else?

MILADY. Yes. I have enemies which I have made in supporting your Grace.

RICHELIEU. Go on.

MILADY. To begin with, there is a scheming little woman called Bonacieux.

RICHELIEU. Yes, she is in prison, under my orders.

MILADY. She was. The Queen obtained an order from the King and had her secretly conveyed to a convent. Your Eminence will kindly tell me where that convent is.

RICHELIEU. You shall know before you leave for England.

MILADY. The other enemy I fear much more than this little wench - her lover, d'Artagnan.

RICHELIEU. He's a bold fellow.

MILADY. Your Grace, let us speak frankly: a fair exchange - life for life, man for man . . . give me one, and I will give you the other.

RICHELIEU. I don't know what you mean, nor do I desire to know. *(He writes.)* But it is said this d'Artagnan is a duelist, and a traitor . . .

MILADY. A notorious villain, Your Grace.

RICHELIEU. Then he should be dealt with accordingly. *(Hands her the paper.)* Your orders ratifying whatever conduct you deem necessary - for the good of France. I will to the King for the information you requested. Wait here and I will send my Guards to escort you to the ship. *(He exits.)*

(Milady folds the writ and puts it away. She attempts to retire in when Athos approaches from behind, and levels his pistol at the back of her head.)

MILADY. Who are you and what do you want?

ATHOS. Turn around. Let me see your face. *(She does.)* Do you recognize me?

MILADY *(A moment).* Count la Fere!

ATHOS. Once before you crossed my path and I thought I'd sent you underground, but I see hell hath brought you back above.

MILADY. What is it you want of me?

ATHOS. Mark me well, Charlotte Backson: murder the Duke of Buckingham or have him murdered, it matters little to me, he's English and an enemy - but if you lay a finger on my friend d'Artagnan, or his mistress, I swear on the soul of my father, I will kill you. Now, give me that paper which the Cardinal signed or upon my soul I will blow your brains out. *(She hesitates. He cocks the gun.)*

MILADY. Take it! And damn your soul!

ATHOS. *(Hearing the return of Richelieu.)* Discover my actions to the Cardinal and I will renounce you for what you really are. I don't think his Eminence would appreciate the courts of Europe knowing he's been keeping company with the regional whore *(He exits. Richelieu enters with two Guards.)*

RICHELIEU. Buckingham has returned to London. You sail for England from Charente. These men will - are you well, Milady? You look ill.

MILADY. I . . . am a little warm.

RICHELIEU. Stay healthy, Madame, the task you have before you may very well decide all our fates. The result of your previous mission has instilled in me a less than enthusiastic confidence in your abilities. I encourage you, this time, Madame, to succeed. *(Milady is quietly livid.)* Ah, your color looks better already; yes . . . revenge offers some consolation even in the mere hope of it, does it not? *(Gestures to his Guards.)* You may go. *(Starts off.)*

MILADY. Your Grace! *(He stops and turns.)* The Bonacieux woman, where is she?

RICHELIEU. The Carmelite convent in Bethune.

(The two Guards escort Milady off. Richelieu retires.)

Scene 29

(Enter Athos, d'Artagnan, Aramis, Porthos, and Planchet elsewhere in camp.)

PORTHOS. I hope, Athos, this news is worth ~~the~~ hearing. I was ~~very nearly asleep~~ almost asleep.

ATHOS. Planchet, stand sentry. Let us know if anyone approaches.

PLANCHET. Can't I have a gun?

D'ART *(d'Art. playfully strikes him and Planchet retires up).* Do as he says.

ATHOS. Over here, gentleman. Porthos, your dice - quickly.

PORTHOS. All this mystery for a game of dice?

ARAMIS. Hold your tongue, Porthos. *(To Athos.)* Why all this secrecy? *(They feign playing a game of dice as they talk.)*

117

ATHOS. I saw Milady. She is here. In camp.

D'ART. Here!?

ATHOS. Yes.

PORTHOS. Would someone please inform me who this *Milady* lady is?

ATHOS *(To Dart)*. For a time, you may breathe easy. She's on her way to England.

D'ART. Why to England?

ATHOS. To assassinate the Duke of Buckingham, or persuade some poor fool to do it for her. I retrieved this from her. *(The writ.)* A blank endorsement extorted from the Cardinal with which this serpent could very well dispatch d'Artagnan, the Duke, and perhaps all of us with impunity.

D'ART. Enemy or not, I say we straight to England and warn the Duke.

ARAMIS. You forget, d'Artagnan, we are at war. Such an act would be treasonous.

ATHOS. I have another idea.

PORTHOS. I was hoping somebody did.

ATHOS. This creature has a brother-in-law, does she not?

D'ART. Yes, Lord de Winter, in England.

ATHOS. He's the man to warn. We will let him know of this monster's intentions - to assassinate their Ambassador - and of her past - it may interest Lord Winter to know she not only wished him dead, but was already married when she wed his brother; therefore she is no longer heir to his fortune.

D'ART. I'll write the letter.

ATHOS *(To d'Art)*. My boy, handle the musket and the sword, but pass the pen to Aramis. That is his province.

PORTHOS *(Incredulously).* Yes, he writes *theses* in Latin.

D'ART. Very well.

ARAMIS *(Taking out his writing kit).* But who shall carry the letter to England? None of us can leave camp without being charged as deserters? *(A beat. They all turn toward Planchet, who is asleep at sentry duty.)*

D'ART. Of course! Planchet knows the way already.

ATHOS. Yes, but is he devoted enough to undertake such a dangerous venture?

D'ART. No, but he loves money more than any man I know.

ATHOS. Very well. *(To Aramis.)* Now for the letter. *(He begins to write.)*

D'ART. Say . . . your sister-in-law sought your death in order to inherit your wealth. Also, that she was never legally married to your brother because she . . .

ATHOS. Because she had already been married in France. And that her husband subsequently discovered a fleur-de-lis branded on her shoulder.

ARAMIS *(Writing).* And who has seen this fleur-de-lis?

ATHOS. d'Artagnan . . . and I. *(Aramis stops writing and looks at Athos.)* Or to observe the proper chronological order, I and d'Artagnan.

PORTHOS. My God! Does the husband of this frightful creature still live?

ATHOS. He lives.

ARAMIS. You are sure?

ATHOS. Yes.

PORTHOS. Can we find him?

ATHOS. I am he. *(A pause of dead silence.)*

ARAMIS. Come, Athos, we will finish the letter in private. *(They exit.)*

D'ART. PLANCHET! *(Planchet wakes, half asleep.)* PLANCHET!

PLANCHET. Messieurs! I only had one bottle! The Anjou! Upon my honor! I - !

D'ART. Planchet! Come with us. You are about to make your fortune.

PLANCHET. Yes, sir. Of course. Whatever you wish, sir. *(They start to exit.)*

PORTHOS. Then it was you took my last bottle of Anjou! You wretch! You miscreant! You stealer of other men's wine!

(They exit.)

Scene 30

(Lord de Winter's Palace. Milady escorted by an officer and guards.)

MILADY. I demand, sir, to know the meaning of this! Who are you and what is your business with me?! In the name of heaven, tell me what this means! If I am a prisoner, what crime have I committed!?

WINTER *(Entering)*. Perhaps *you* can enlighten us on that subject, sister.

MILADY. My . . . Lord de Winter . . . what is the meaning of this?!

WINTER. Leave us. Post two guards outside the door, and summon my steward. *(The guards exits.)* Let us chat, shall we?

MILADY. Please.

WINTER. Very Well. So, tell me, dear sister, what brings you so suddenly to England?

MILADY. Why to see you, brother!

WINTER. Oh, it was for my sake alone that you took the trouble to cross the channel in time of war. How flattering.

MILADY. I am your nearest of kin, am I not?

WINTER. And so my only heir, are you not?

MILADY. What do you mean by such a question, my lord?

WINTER. You came here, you said, to see me? Well, Madame, you shall see me everyday.

MILADY. I am your prisoner then?

WINTER. Very observant, Madame. If you are not comfortable here, simply tell me how your *first* husband furnished your household and I will endeavor to do the same.

MILADY. My first husband?!

WINTER. In the mean time, I advise you to endure your captivity in quiet. After the Duke of Buckingham arrives to sign the papers, you will be exiled. If you try to escape you will be executed. And if I ever prove that you had a hand in my brother's death, I swear on his soul, I will hunt you down and kill you myself. *(A knock at the door.)* Enter. Ah, Mr. Felton. As you are in charge of this woman, I wanted you to look at her. Carefully. She is young and beautiful, I know - but under that thin veneer of beauty she harbors a depraved and corrupted soul. Swear by your own hopes of salvation to preserve this wretched creature for the punishment she deserves.

FELTON. I swear that all shall be done as you desire.

WINTER. And now, Madame, I advise you to make your peace with God, for men have passed their judgment on you already. *(He exits.)*

FELTON. You will sleep in the room beyond. You will be served meals three time a day.

MILADY. I thank you, sir. I . . . I . . . *(Milady fakes fainting. Felton does not react. Winter walks in right away, obviously having been at the door.)*

FELTON. She seems to have fainted, my lord.

WINTER. I told you she would, didn't I? This is only the first act of her comedy. Come, John, you Puritans may frown upon theater, but, I assure you, this is as fine a performance as you'll ever see. Adieu, my dear sister, until your next *swoon*. *(They exit.)*

MILADY *(Sitting up)*. A Puritan!

Scene 31

(A road at the camp of La Rochelle. The three musketeers and d'Artagnan.)

PORTHOS. Really, gentlemen, you're acting like children to let a woman frighten you so.

ATHOS. She's no woman; that thing has no soul.

D'ART. Planchet will be here. I have great faith in the fellow - and the purse of gold awaiting his return.

ARAMIS. And if he doesn't come?

D'ART. It's a lengthy trip to London and back, any number of things could have stayed his return.

ARAMIS *(Seeing Planchet)*. Someone's coming!

D'ART. Is it he!?

PLANCHET. It is.

D'ART. Planchet!

ARAMIS AND PORTHOS. Planchet!

PLANCHET. Why do you all look so astonished?

PORTHOS. We thought perhaps you were . . . well . . . dead, actually.

D'ART. Why were you delayed?

PLANCHET. The English navy, sir. They stopped our ship in the harbor and interrogated everyone on board - they lined us up to be searched. I snuck back to my cabin, though, and sewed the letter into the lining of my coat.

D'ART. Well done.

PLANCHET. I completed my mission, Monsieur. And have carried back a reply.

D'ART *(Taking the note. They all huddle around to read).* "Thank you. Rest easy."

ARAMIS *(Seeing Richelieu).* The Cardinal!

(Richelieu and two or three of his guards enter unexpectedly. The musketeers and d'Art. Aramis hide the note. All jump to attention)

RICHELIEU. Are the English expected by land, gentlemen, that I find you so far from the siege?

ATHOS. Pardon us, Monsignor, but being off duty we assumed we could spend our time as we pleased.

RICHELIEU. Do you know what you look like, gentlemen? Always together, always armed? You look like four conspirators.

ATHOS. We do conspire, Your Grace, against all enemies of France.

RICHELIEU. Indeed? Then I'm sure you wouldn't mind letting me read the letter which you so hastily hid when I approached. Monsieur Aramis, the letter, please.

ARAMIS. Your Holiness, forgive me, but it is a letter from a woman.

RICHELIEU. Ah, yes, we must be discreet about such things. Nevertheless it can be shown to a confessor, and as you know I, for one, have *taken* my Holy Orders.

ATHOS *(Stepping in, face to face with the Cardinal).* Your Grace, the letter is from a woman, but rest assured, it is not signed by any of the many ladies so ignobly rumored to be one of your mistresses.

(A tense beat. Richelieu, quietly furious. All are ready for a fight. Richelieu assesses the situation, contains his anger and smiles.)

RICHELIEU. You are brave men, proud in the daylight and loyal in darkness. If there were danger to be feared on the road I am about to take, I would want none other than you to accompany me, but since I do not fear, and you are off duty, enjoy your day . . . and your letter. Adieu, Gentlemen.

ALL. Your Grace. *(They all bow. Richelieu and his men exit.)*

D'ART. That letter must be burned.

PORTHOS. I have a better idea. Planchet, as punishment for being late you shall be so kind as to eat this paper. And to reward the great service you have done us, you may wash it down with a bottle of wine. *(Putting it in his mouth.)* Eat heartily now.

PLANCHET. Yes, Monsieur!

(He eats, anxious to get the wine. They exit.)

Scene 32

(De Winter's Castle. Milady runs on and listens at the door. She hears Felton coming and quickly runs center, kneels and prays. Felton enters with food for her and watches from the doorway. He locks the door.)

MILADY. I am in the hand of my enemies, oh Lord. Grant me the strength to suffer this persecution with dignity. Lord, send me, if am worthy, a savior, for many they are that fight against me, or let me die for you. *(Feigning surprise in noticing Felton.)* Sir, you frightened me.

FELTON. Your dinner, Madame.

MILADY. I will not eat.

FELTON. Very well, Madame. *(He starts out.)*

MILADY *(Thinking quick, she takes out a bible).* And take this with you! Lord de Winter knows perfectly well I am not of his religion, and yet he must torment me each day by thrusting his *Catholic* bible at me!

FELTON. What religion is it you profess, Madame?

MILADY. I will declare that on the day that I have suffered enough for my faith. *(Flings the bible at him.)* Carry that away and make use of it yourself. *(Felton begins to exit. Milady begins sings a Puritan psalm.)* "I'll put my trust in thee, what time I am afraid, In God I'll praise his word, In God My confidence have stayed."

FELTON. Madame, what is that you sing?

MILADY. I crave your pardon, sir. I forgot such songs are out of place in such a house. Oh, lord, forgive this man as I myself forgive him.

FELTON.   Forgive me, Madame?   I have done
nothing. Whatever it is you are guilty of, you must submit
to heaven and ask forgiveness.

MILADY.   What I am guilty of?!   P   You poor
foolish man, you know not what you do.

FELTON.   You say either too much, or two little,
Madame. Tell me what it is you mean. I am your brother
in faith.

MILADY. You?! My brother in faith and yet you
will turn me over to the enemy of England, the enemy of
God! My brother, and yet you would deliver me unto that
blasphemous heretic!

FELTON. Who is it you speak of?

MILADY. Having eyes, see you not? Having ears,
hear you not?

FELTON. What mean you by this, Madame?

MILADY.   Oh, you would have me confide my
shame to you? A man? Never, never could I do that.

FELTON. Madame, I ask nothing but -

MILADY. Shall I dare trust myself to you? I would
rather die, here, innocent for my faith than suffer yet
another betrayal.

FELTON. I swear I will not betray you or our faith.

MILADY. When I was very young I was persecuted
for practicing my faith. I resisted. And since my
persecutor could not make me lose my soul, he determined
to defile my body.

FELTON. You mean . . . ?

MILADY. He took by force the thing he could not
overcome by torture. I fought back, brother, I did! Before
God, I was not willing! but my strength was no match for
his...when I awoke, I was in his chambers, my clothes . . .

torn from me and strewn about the room. *(She breaks down.)*

FELTON. Oh, sister. Who was this villain!?

MILADY. When I . . . when he returned I threatened to reveal his horrible crime to the world. To silence me he summoned his executioner - who did this to me! *(She rips down the top of her dress revealing the fleur-de-lis.)* Yes! Branded for life like some . . . some - I cannot bring myself to speak the word.

FELTON. But who, Madame!? Who did this to you!?

MILADY. Need I say his name? The man who is devastating England, who persecutes the Puritans, a man who puts his country at war to satisfy his own lustful whims!

FELTON. The Duke of Buckingham!? It's Buckingham!?

MILADY. It is he himself who signs the orders for my exile. *(She grabs Felton's knife and tries to stab herself. Felton stops her.)* Oh, let me die, sir! Please, I beg of you! *(There is banging on the door.)* Leave your knife and lock the door. I will do the rest!

WINTER *(From outside).* Felton! Felton, open this door! John! *(Felton opens the door.)* What's going on in here?

MILADY. Tell him! Tell him what I wanted from you!

WINTER. John?

FELTON. She asked that I give her my knife.

WINTER. Why, is there someone whose throat she'd like to cut?

MILADY. There is myself. And my God would surely forgive me for the act.

WINTER. Your *God?* What have we decided to indulge in a bit of apostasy now?

MILADY *(Singing a psalm again)*. "Mine enemies they would swallow me up daily, for they be many that do fight against thee, O most high."

WINTER. Upon my honor, I think the vixen's finally gone mad.

MILADY. You insult me, my God, and my faith!

WINTER. Is it really possible to insult you, Madame? *(Milady prays fervently.)* Well, my lady *Puritan,* pray all you want. It'll do you little good for your earthly crimes, but may redeem you elsewhere. Come John, you have been in here too long. John!

FELTON. But, my lord -

WINTER. Leave the room, John, I command you.

FELTON. Yes, My lord. *(He exits.)*

WINTER. Madame, I leave you to your prayers. The Duke has arrived to sign the papers in your presence, after which, we and England will be rid of you forever. *(He exits.)*

MILADY. Damn him! I was so close! *(We hear keys in the door.)* Who's there?

FELTON *(From outside)*. Shh!

MILADY. Oh, God, is it possible?

FELTON *(Coming in with a rope ladder)*. Quickly. Madame, there's no time to lose.

MILADY. Oh, Felton, the Lord is truly on our side.

FELTON. This is all the gold I have at present. *(He puts it down.)* It should be enough for us to charter a vessel for us. Where shall we say we are going?

MILADY *(Taking a short beat to think)*. Once in France, there is a town called Bethune. I know some people there. I'm sure they will take us in.

FELTON.   Very well. *(We hear others approaching.)*
Hurry!
MILADY. Wait! The gold!

*(She runs for the gold but it is too late. Winter,
Buckingham, Patrick, and Officer all enter the room.
Felton conceals himself, behind the door, or somewhere
else behind the Duke.)*

WINTER. This is she, my Lord.
MILADY. Your Grace.
BUCK. Grace me no Grace, as the poet says.
WINTER *(Handing the orders of exile).* The papers, my
lord.
BUCK.   Madame, having heard the details of your
past and present crimes, I can only say that you are being
treated quite mercifully in having your punishment limited
only to exile. Take a step on English ground again and I
will have you drawn and quartered. You are now,
Madame, in the hands of God.
MILADY *(Seeing Felton advancing, knife in hand).* As are
you, my Lord.
WINTER *(Overlapping).* Felton!!
FELTON *(As he stabs Duke. Overlapping).* Oh, ever
loving God, guide my hand -
BUCK *(Felton stabs the Duke. Overlapping).* God! Help!
Help!
FELTON. Avenge our brethren!

*(Amid the yelling and chaos, Milady runs for the window
and escapes. They subdue Felton.)*

WINTER *(To Felton)*. You miserable wretch ! What have you done!?

FELTON. Only what God has willed.

WINTER. What God has willed? You blasted fool, that accursed she-devil willed it, not your God! After her! Quickly!

PATRICK *(At the Duke's body)*. His Grace is dead. The Duke of Buckingham is dead.

WINTER. Merciful heaven . . . what have we done? *(They exit.)*

Scene 33

(France.   The siege at La Rochelle.   The three musketeers, d'Artagnan, and Treville.)

TREVILLE. Gentlemen, the King grows weary of the siege and wants for a diversion. He has resolved, therefore, to travel to Saint-Germaine and partake in the festival of St. Louis. Athos, gather me twenty men to escort the King. *(Sounds offstage.)* What noise is this? Aramis, go and find out. *(Aramis starts out, the Cardinal enters. The men stand at attention.)*

RICHELIEU *(Entering with Guards)*. Monsieur Treville, the Kings excursion to Saint-Germain has been canceled. We have just received somewhat shocking news from England. The Duke of Buckingham is dead. Murdered by one of his own countryman in the Castle of Lord de Winter.

D'ART. My God.

ATHOS. Shh!

TREVILLE. Are you sure the information is reliable?

RICHELIEU. Quite sure, Captain, it comes from an eyewitness arrived in France this morning.

TREVILLE. May I speak with him?

RICHELIEU. *Her*, Monsieur. A woman recently escaped from wrongful imprisonment under the hands of that libertine Buckingham - God rest his soul. At present, she is being safe-conducted to Bethune. Treville, The King waits upon us. *(Treville and Richelieu exit.)*

ATHOS. Bethune?

D'ART. Constance. To horse, gentlemen! To horse! *(They all rush off.)*

Scene 34

(The convent at Bethune. One or two nuns are present doing busy work, as is the Mother Superior. Rochefort enters with Milady. A few Guards linger behind.)

MILADY *(To Roche)*. Remember: treat me harshly. I shall not be long. Wait for me here.

NUN *(Seeing them)*. Good day to you. May I help you?

ROCHE. By order of the Cardinal. *(Hands her a paper.)* She is to be confined here until further notice. *(He pushes Milady into the room.)*

NUN. May I know, sir, what if any - ?

ROCHE. You know all that you need to know. Good day.

NUN. You poor child. *(To the other nuns who are watching.)* Sisters, leave us. Come, dear, you need fear nothing here. God is with you and will protect you.

MILADY. Please don't hurt me.

NUN. Hurt you? My sweet girl, no one will hurt you here.

MILADY. But you are . . . of the church - the Cardinal's church.

NUN. The Cardinal and the church are two very different things, my dear. Come, stand up. I tell you, you are safe here. Though I am little acquainted with worldly concerns, I have seen more than one example of such persecution by Monsieur le Cardinal. We have a young lady with us now that has suffered much under his vengeance. You are not an enemy of the Church?

MILADY. I?! No! God bears me witness, I am a devout Catholic! The only crime I committed was . . . I am so ashamed - was to spurn an unwanted invitation from the Cardinal to . . . I cannot speak it . . . I . . . *(She breaks down.)*

NUN *(Comforting her).* My poor child . . . say no more. Shhh . . . you're safe here. Come, you must be tired from your journey. Rest here while I prepare a room for you.

MILADY *(Kissing her hand).* Thank you, sister.

NUN. I will send you some supper. *(She exits.)*

ROCHE *(Entering).* Milady!

MILADY. Get out of here, you fool! You'll ruin everything!

ROCHE. We must leave at once! The guards on the road report four or five men approaching at a gallop.

MILADY. Hold them off. I don't need much time.

ROCHE. Milady, it were better to - *(Milady hears someone approaching.)*

MILADY. Do as I say! *(Rochefort runs off. Constance enters.)*

CONSTANCE *(To Milady)*.   The Mother Superior asked me to bring you something to eat.

MILADY *(Aside)*.   How fate loves a jest.

CONSTANCE.   Forgive me, but I wasn't told your name.

MILADY.   Anne de Beuil.   *(To Constance.)*   And yours, my sweet friend?

CONSTANCE.   Constance Bonacieux.

MILADY.   What a pretty name.

CONSTANCE.   Is it true, what the Mother Superior tells me, that you too are persecuted by this wicked priest the Cardinal?

MILADY.   Shh!   Even here, we must be careful of what we say.

CONSTANCE.   Forgive me.   I've been here so long without the slightest diversion.   And now, to see another in the same plight as myself!   *(Milady comforts her.)*

MILADY.   We must all put our trust in heaven, my child.   There will come a time when the good we have done will plead our case before God.   We must find solace in that.

CONSTANCE.   Forgive me, my friend, it is you who need comfort now, not I.   *(Gathering herself.)*   A glass of wine, Madame?

MILADY.   If you would be so kind as to join me. *(Milady takes the glasses, as Constance goes for the bottle.   Milady pours poison into Constance's cup.)*

CONSTANCE.   I am not without friends, and perhaps, once they come for me, I can be of some help to you.

MILADY *(As Constance pours the wine)*.   Are you sure they will come for you?

CONSTANCE. Oh yes, when it is safe. They will come. I am sure of it.

MILADY. How fortunate you are. I have no one who will come for me. *(Holding up their glasses.)* To our deliverance, Madame.

CONSTANCE. Perhaps it is fate that we have met here.

MILADY. Perhaps it is. *(They drink.)*

(We hear a commotion outside. Men yelling, swords clashing, a musket shot or two.)

ROCHE *(Running on with a guard or two)*. Milady, come with me now or you're lost!

CONSTANCE *(Recognizing him)*. You!

ROCHE *(To Milady)*. Milady, we must withdraw at once!

CONSTANCE. My lady Anne, that man, he . . . *(She is starting to feel the effects of the poison.)* . . . go not with him . . . he . . . *(The Mother Superior and a nun enter.)*

MILADY *(Overlapping and ignoring Constance)*. Is it them? The musketeers?

ROCHE. Yes, Madame, and Monsieur d'Artagnan.

MILADY. Stay and kill him, but not before he sees her die!

ROCHE *(To his guards)*. Take her away! *(The guards exit with Milady. d'Art. runs on with two or three other musketeers - not Athos, Aramis or Porthos.)*

NUN *(To Rochefort)*. What is the meaning of this, sir?!

D'ART. It *is* him! Hold, gentlemen! He is mine! After Milady! *(The musketeers exit.)*

CONSTANCE. d'Artagnan, is that you? Is it?!

D'ART.   Constance, stay where you are!   *(To Rochefort.)*   Have you no where to run this time, you coward!

ROCHE. You would be the wiser to run, sir.

D'ART. I think not.

(d'Artagnan attacks Rochefort. They fight. Close to the end of the fight, Porthos, Athos, Aramis, and Planchet enter, swords out, pistol in hand. d'Artagnan kills Rochefort.)

ROCHE *(After he is mortally wounded. To d'Artagnan).* Commend me to the Cardinal.

D'ART. Commend me to Satan.

CONSTANCE *(Stumbles into his arms)* d'Artagnan . . .

D'ART. Constance, what is it? What's the matter?

NUN. She is not well, sir.

D'ART *(To Constance).* Constance, we've come to - *(Constance collapses in his arms.)* . . . oh my God, help! . . . help, Athos, her hands are ice cold . . . she's fainted . . .

ATHOS *(To d'Art).* Porthos, some water. *(Porthos goes off with a sister for water. Athos goes for the wine glasses to put the water in. He looks in the glass, fingers the resin in the bottom of the glass and devines what has happened.)*

D'ART. Constance. Constance, can you hear me!?

ARAMIS *(To Athos).* What's this? *(Athos shows him the resin.)*

D'ART. She's alive! Thank you, God!

CONSTANCE. Is that you d'Artagnan? *(Porthos comes back on with water.)*

ATHOS *(To Constance).* Madame, in the name of heaven, whose was this empty glass?

CONSTANCE. Mine, Monsieur.

D'ART. What is it, Athos?

ATHOS *(To Constance)*. And who poured the wine that was in it?

CONSTANCE. The lady . . . the pretty lady . . . she . . . *(Starts to fade.)*

D'ART. Athos, help me! She's cold again!

CONSTANCE *(Calmly)*. Yes . . . yes. I'm cold, d'Artagnan. *(She dies. The sisters pray.)*

D'ART. Someone run and call for help! Aramis, Porthos! My friends, in the name of God, someone help me!! *(All know there is nothing they can do.)* Constance. Constance . . .

ATHOS. Weep, my poor heart. *(Walking away.)* Would that I could weep as you. My heart is as cold as she.

PLANCHET *(Comforting d'Artagnan)*. Master?

ARAMIS. Athos, we should after Milady.

ATHOS. Let the boy have a moment to mourn; revenge will keep. *(Seeing Porthos who is quite moved.)* Porthos, courage, now, yes? *(Porthos nods his head yes. Lord Winter enters with Patrick. The Musketeers draw on him.)* Who are you, sir?

WINTER. A friend.

PLANCHET. It's the Lord de Winter.

WINTER. Yes. *(Seeing the body.)* I come in search of a woman whom I assume has passed through here . . . for I see her handiwork.

ATHOS. She cannot be far. You and your man can assist us, if you wish.

WINTER. I am at your service, sir.

MUSKETEER 4 *(Entering. To Athos)*. We have her! In the park behind the convent!

ATHOS *(To the Mother Superior).* Sister, we abandon to your care the body of this unfortunate woman. *(To d'Art.)* Come, d'Artagnan. Come. *(To all of Milady.)*

WINTER. Sir, if there are any measures to be taken against this woman, I should like to be have a voice. She is my sister-in-law.

ATHOS. Sir, she is my wife. You will follow. Aramis, pen and paper. Planchet! d'Artagnan, give me that letter of the Cardinal's. *(d'Art. gives it to Athos. Athos gives it to Planchet.)* Planchet, take this and guard it with your life. *(Athos writes.)* Go to this address. Find the man that lives there and bring him to us. If he refuses, show him the Cardinal's letter. *(To the rest.)* Gentlemen, follow me.

(They all exit.)

Scene 35

(A field behind the convent. Milady enters, held by two guards. Her hands are bound behind her back. Her dress is torn. Her hair disheveled.)

MILADY *(To the guards).* Before God, gentlemen, I am guilty of no crime! I am here persecuted by the Cardinal for my loyalty to the Queen! Help, my friends! *(They don't respond.)* A thousand pistoles for each of you if you help me escape. I have friends that will make our fortune if you will assist me! Two thousand! *(They don't respond.)* You are both dead, I swear to God, you're dead if you deliver me up to these men. I have friends who will

make you pay dearly for any harm that comes to me!
(Athos enters.)
ATHOS. Let her be, gentlemen.

(The men let her go. Athos takes a step toward her and she runs toward an exit. Porthos and Aramis enter from that exit. She runs to another. De Winter and Patrick enter from that exit. She runs to another and d'Artagnan enters in that one. She retreats.. d'Artagnan does not stop, he keeps approaching her, draws his pistol and levels it at Milady's head. Athos steps in.)

ATHOS. Put it down. She will be judged, not murdered. Wait but a little and you shall be satisfied. *(d'Art. backs off.)*
MILADY. What is it you want?!
ATHOS. We want Charlotte Backson, who was first called the Countess de la Fere, and afterwards Lady de Winter.
MILADY. I am she. What is it you want with me!?
ATHOS. To judge you according to your crimes.
MILADY. Who are you to presume to judge me?
ATHOS. Before God and before men, I swear that I married this woman when she was a young girl only to discover that she was plotting my death in order to inherit my fortune.
WINTER. Before God and before men, I accuse this woman of having devised the murder of my brother, her husband, and of having caused the death of The Duke of Buckingham, and the subsequent execution of his assassin, John Felton.
ATHOS. Monsieur d'Artagnan.

D'ART. Before God and before men, I accuse this woman of having murdered Constance Bonacieux.

ATHOS, ARAMIS, AND PORTHOS. We bear witness to that.

ATHOS. Monsieur d'Artagnan, what is the penalty you demand for this woman?

D'ART. Death.

ATHOS. Lord de Winter.

WINTER. Death.

ATHOS. Messieurs Porthos and Aramis, you are judges too. What penalty do you demand?

BOTH. Death.

ATHOS. Your crimes have wearied men on earth and God in heaven. If you know any prayers, say them now.

(Planchet enters with the executioner, wrapped in a great red cloak. Milady does not see him.)

MILADY. You cowards! It takes you ten men to kill one woman!

ATHOS. You're not a woman; you don't belong to the human species.

MILADY. Oh, yes! You are all such virtuous men! Please you to remember, he that touches a hair on my head is a murderer and an enemy of the state! My actions were authorized, and for the good of France. You cannot carry out this sentence yourself!

ATHOS. True, Madame. But the public executioner can. *(Athos gestures to the executioner.)*

MILADY. Under whose authority!?

ATHOS. Why, Madame, under the authority of Cardinal Richelieu himself. Planchet.

MILADY. You're mad!

ATHOS *(Planchet gives him the Cardinal's letter. Athos holds it up to her).* Perhaps you remember this paper, Madame? The one I took from you? *(Reads it.)* "It is by my order and for the good of France that the bearer of this paper has done what he has done." Signed: Armand-Jean Duplessis, Cardinal-Duc de Richelieu." And his seal. *(Athos gestures to the executioner. He comes toward Milady.)*

MILADY *(Falling to her knees).* If I am guilty, let me be judged in a court of law! You are not judges! You cannot condemn me!

EXECUTIONER. Come.

MILADY. God in heaven, won't someone help me!

D'ART. Athos . . . perhaps we are wrong in this. Should we not bring her back to -

ATHOS *(Athos draws his sword).* Another step and, dearly as I love you, we fight. *(d'Art. hesitates.)* All for one . . . and . . . one for all. *(d'Art. relents.)* Come, Executioner, to your charge.

MILADY. Will no one help me?! *(No one responds. The Executioner attempts to help her up. She shrugs him off and rises in a flash. She looks her accuser's in the eye. Then, to the Executioner.)* Where am I to die?

(The executioner walks her to the place of execution. Milady stops and faces the men.)

ATHOS. May you die in peace.

MILADY. May you die.

(She pulls the hair off of her neck, turns, kneels, and presents her neck to the blade of the executioner. He lifts the sword above his head.)

ATHOS. God's justice be done.

(The sword falls. All exit.)

Scene 36

(The house of Monsieur Treville. Musketeers busy preparing for the induction of d'Artagnan into the Musketeers. They set a place for the King and Queen to sit. Treville enters reading a letter.)

TREVILLE. Gentlemen. Gentlemen! A moment, please. *(The Musketeers stops and stand at attention.)* The siege is ended. La Rochelle has surrendered! *(The Musketeers cheer. Reading.)* A fitting vanguard to this day. *(d'Artagnan, Athos, Porthos, and Aramis enter. d'Artagnan no longer wears the uniform of Dessarts Guards. He is in a doublet, or shirt. Athos holds his sword.)* Ah, my friends. *(They stand at attention.)* All is in order. The King shall arrive shortly. Heard you the news?

ATHOS. Sir?

TREVILLE. The siege is ended. We shall not be returning to La Rochelle. Athos, a word with you. *(Treville and Athos cross up and speak.)*

PORTHOS. *(To d'Artagnan.)* Are they serving food here today?

(The Cardinal and four or five of his guards enter. The guards immediately train their muskets on d'Artagnan, Aramis, Porthos, Athos and Treville. The Musketeers all react, going for their swords.)

TREVILLE *(Calling for his men to stand down).* Gentlemen! Gentlemen! *(It's a stand off. To the Cardinal.)* May I ask, sir, the meaning of this unexpected visit?

RICHELIEU. Pardon me for interrupting, Monsieur, but I'm afraid I have to place one of your musketeers under arrest. Monsieur d'Artagnan, if you will please come with me.

(d'Artagnan steps forward. The Musketeers react. d'Artagnan gestures to them to stand down.)

D'ART *(Calmly).* Would your Grace be so good as to inform me as to what crimes I am charged withal?

RICHELIEU. Monsieur d'Artagnan is charged with having conspired with the enemies of this Kingdom, having intercepted state secrets, and of conspiring and partaking in an unlawful execution.

D'ART. But, Your Grace, I have already been pardoned of these actions.

RICHELIEU *(Contemptuously).* Pardoned!? By whom - the King?!

D'ART. No, sir. By Your Eminence.

RICHELIEU. By me?! Are you mad, Monsieur!?

D'ART *(Holding out the letter).* Monsignor will doubtless recognize his own handwriting.

RICHELIEU *(Snatching the letter and reading it).* "It is by my order and for the good of France that the bearer of this paper -" *(The Cardinal realizes he has been trumped. He looks up at d'Artagnan. He turns and walks away for a moment.)*

PORTHOS *(To d'Art).* I believe he's meditating on what sort of torture he will use on you.

D'ART. I assure you, my friend, I do not hold life so dear as to be afraid of death.

RICHELIEU *(Turning back).* Monsieur . . . *(Approaches D'art. Privately.)* . . . I do wish you worked for me. *(He gestures for his men to stand down.)* Captain Treville, please forgive me for this misunderstanding. *(We hear the King approaching.)* I would be honored to remain and add to the names endorsing this young man's commission.

TREVILLE *(Politely).* Your Grace.

(The King and Queen enter, attended. All on stage take their formal place for the ceremony.)

KING *(To the Cardinal).* Your Grace, a pleasure as always. I did not expect your presence.

RICHELIEU. I was fortunate enough to be in the vicinity, Sire. *(To the Queen.)* Your Majesty.

(Anne deigns Richelieu a nod of her head as she passes him. The King and Queen take their positions, as does the rest of those present. Treville hands the King a document.)

KING. Monsieur d'Artagnan. *(d'Art. steps forward and kneels before the King.)*

ANNE. Sir, Ourself and our nation express our gratitude and hold you in great esteem for your efforts on behalf of your Queen . . . and King.

KING. Rise, sir. Upon recommendation of Captain Treville, Captain Dessart of the Royal Guards, and Her Majesty the Queen, you are hereby granted a lieutenant's commission in the King's Royal Musketeers. *(Treville steps forward and places the uniform of a Musketeer on d'Art.)* You justly deserve the uniform you wear. Gentlemen.

ARAMIS. Your lieutenancy, cost me many a prayer, my friend.

D'ART. Of which I am indeed grateful, my dear Aramis.

PLANCHET. Do I get paid, now?

D'ART. Yes, you do.

PORTHOS. Do we have to address you as Lieutenant, now?

D'ART. Yes, you do.

PORTHOS. Damn!

ARAMIS. Porthos, I really must convert you, you know.

PORTHOS. Oh, good God.

ARAMIS. That's a beginning.

ATHOS *(Handing him his sword)*. Congratulations. You're a Musketeer.

D'ART. Yes. I longed for the day. Now it is here . . . I feel nothing.

ATHOS. You're young. There's time for you to feel again. Come on, now. *(Calling out.)* Aramis! Porthos! . . . Planchet! *(They come together.)* All for one . . . *(He looks to d'Art.)*

D'ART. *(Begins this last line, and then the rest join in.)* And one for all!

(The end.)

MUSIC USE NOTE

Licensees are solely responsible for obtaining formal written permission from copyright owners to use copyrighted music in the performance of this play and are strongly cautioned to do so. If no such permission is obtained by the licensee, then the licensee must use only original music that the licensee owns and controls. Licensees are solely responsible and liable for all music clearances and shall indemnify the copyright owners of the play(s) and their licensing agent, Samuel French, against any costs, expenses, losses and liabilities arising from the use of music by licensees. Please contact the appropriate music licensing authority in your territory for the rights to any incidental music.

IMPORTANT BILLING AND CREDIT REQUIREMENTS

If you have obtained performance rights to this title, please refer to your licensing agreement for important billing and credit requirements.